魯迅小說集詞彙
Lu Xün Xiǎo Shuō Jí: Vocabulary
(Selected Short Stories of Lu Xün)

魯迅小說集詞彙

Lu Xùn Xiǎo Shuō Jí:
Vocabulary
(Selected Short Stories of Lu Xùn)

魯迅小說集詞彙
Lu Xün Xiǎo Shuō Jí: Vocabulary
(Selected Short Stories of Lu Xün)

Translated by D.C. Lau

中文大學出版社
The Chinese University Press
Hong Kong

International Standard Book Number: 962-201-185-3

The Chinese University Press
SHATIN, N.T., HONG KONG

*Exclusively distributed in North America by
Cheng & Tsui Co., P. O. Box 328, Cambridge,
MA. 02139, U.S.A.*

Typesetting and Printing by Friendship Printing Co. Ltd., Hong Kong

Contents

Contents

Introduction

Over a period of almost thirty years during which I taught Chinese to English students, I became more and more convinced that the real obstacle to reasonable progress was the lack of adequate learning aids. To begin with, there are no reliable dictionaries, whether for the classical language or the modern. None of the available dictionaries deserve the name. All that they do is to give a list of English equivalents with little indication of how a word is actually used. All the student can do when consulting a dictionary is to choose an equivalent which he suspects to be the one required by the context of what he is reading. More often than not the choice is wrong.* When I first took on the reading of some Lu Xün short stories with my students I discovered that it took them, on average, some four hours of preparation for each hour in class. If the result was satisfactory, perhaps the time and drudgery might have been justified. But the results were, in fact, far from satisfactory. First, the choice made by the student may be wrong. Second and more serious, the equivalents given in the dictionary may themselves be ill-chosen. It has become a kind of dogma that a foreign language should not be learned through translation, but this is, at best, a counsel of perfection. With the limited amount of time available for learning a foreign language, often in adverse linguistic environment, the student has no alternative but to rely heavily on translation. Thus the equivalent a student finds in a dictionary in the initial stages of his learning process often stays firmly associated with the original word in his mind, and it takes a great deal of effort to eradicate this association. For instance, more generations of students than I care to remember have automatically translated the word *xian* 賢 as 'worthy'. Even apart from the inaccuracy of the equivalent, 'worthy' is hardly a living word in the English language outside set expressions like 'a worthy cause' and can mean little to the modern reader. Again, *yüan* 怨 is almost always rendered 'resent'. Although 'resent' conveys something of the meaning of the original word, the feeling is totally different. Such equivalents, once fixed firmly in the minds of the learner, will constitute a serious obstacle to his full understanding of the words in question. This is a grave defect in existing Chinese-English dictionaries.

For a number of years I taught Lu Xün stories to second year students.

*The situation is somewhat changed with the publication in 1979 of *The Chinese-English Dictionary* (Hong Kong: The Commercial Press, Ltd.).

After a year or two I came to feel that no useful purpose was served by subjecting students, year after year, to the gruelling task of looking up every word in inadequate dictionaries. I compiled a vocabulary for the Preface to *Na Han* together with ten stories, eight from *Na Han* and two from *Pang Huang*. My practice was to choose English equivalents which not only can be used in translating the passage concerned but also will not be a false equivalent the student will have to unlearn in subsequent years. Where the meaning in the context is somewhat specialised the more general meaning is added afterwards after a semicolon. From time to time I feel it necessary to give some indication of the level of speech. In such cases, some epithet such as 'literary', 'formal', 'informal' or 'humorous' is added.

The greatest handicap a beginner in Chinese has to work under is that, unlike his colleagues studying a modern European language, he has no fully annotated text he can read after he has mastered the rudiments of the language. This volume, it is hoped, will fill such a gap. Anyone who has done a year of elementary Chinese should have no difficulty working through the text with practically no need to refer to the dictionary. If it helps, in the least way, to take away some of the frustration and drudgery from the learning of modern Chinese, the compiler will feel amply rewarded.

Hong Kong   D. C. Lau
May 1979

The Romanization used is standard pinyin except that the umlaut sign is always inserted for the sake of clarity. The pronunciation used follows that given in the *Xiandai Hanyu Cidian* (Hong Kong, 1977) and differs at times from pronunciation given in older dictionaries as the *Xiandai Hanyu Cidian* incorporates the decisions on the standardization of the pronunciation of a large number of compounds taken by the Putonghua Shenyin Weiyuanhui and published in 1963.

自序

　　我在年青時候也曾經做過許多夢，後來大半忘卻了，但自己也並不以爲可惜。所謂回憶者，雖說可以使人歡欣，有時也不免使人寂寞，使精神的絲縷還牽着已逝的寂寞的時光，又有什麼意味呢，而我偏苦于不能全忘卻，這不能全忘的一部分，到現在便成了《吶喊》的來由。

　　我有四年多，曾經常常，——幾乎是每天，出入于質鋪和藥店裏，年紀可是忘卻了，總之是藥店的櫃臺正和我一樣高，質鋪的是比我高一倍，我從一倍高的櫃臺外送上衣服或首飾去，在侮蔑裏接了錢，再到一樣高的櫃臺上給我久病的父親去買藥。回家之後，又須忙別的事了，因爲開方的醫生是最有名的，以此所用的藥引也奇特：冬天的蘆根，經霜三年的甘蔗，蟋蟀要原對的，結子的平地木，……多不是容易辦到

自序 Zi xü

自序	zìxù	author's preface
曾經	céngjīng (+ verb)	(had) at one time or other (done)
卻	qüè	perfective particle
忘卻	wàngqüè	have quite forgotten
所謂…者	suǒwèi . . . zhě	what is called . . ., what is known as . . ., what goes under the name of . . .
回憶	huíyì	memories, what is recalled to mind
歡欣	huānxīn	joyous
寂寞	jímò	lonely
精神	jīngshén	spirit, mind
絲縷	sīlü	strands
牽	qiān	not free from, tied to, involved with
已	yǐ	(classical) already
已逝	yǐ shì	already gone, passed away
時光	shíguāng	time
意味	yìwèi	point
又有什麼意味呢？		what point is there?
偏	piān	indicating contrariness
苦于	kǔyú	the trouble is
來由	láiyóu	how something comes about
常常	chángcháng	frequently
出入	chūrù	to be in and out of
質鋪	zhìpù	pawn shop
總之	zǒngzhì	at any rate, in short
櫃臺	guìtái	counter
送上	sòng shàng	offer up, pass up
首飾	shǒushì	jewellery
侮蔑	wūmiè	humiliation, insult
須	xü	it is necessary to
開方	kāi fāng	to write out a prescription
藥引	yàoyǐn	the ingredient in a prescription which acts as a catalyst
奇特	qítè	out of the ordinary, out of the way
蘆根	lúgēn	aloe root
經	jīng	to go through, to experinece, to weather
經霜三年的	jīng shuāng sān nián de	that had weathered three years' frost
甘蔗	gānzhè	sugar cane
蟋蟀	xīshuài	cricket
原對	yüánduì	a pair with original partners
結子	jié zǐ	seeds are formed
平地木	píng dì mù	Ardisia (name of a herb)
辦到	bàn daò	to manage

的東西。然而我的父親終于日重一日的亡故了。

　　有誰從小康人家而墜入困頓的麼，我以爲在這途路中，大概可以看見世人的眞面目；我要到N進K學堂去了，彷彿是想走異路，逃異地，去尋求別樣的人們。我的母親沒有法，辦了八元的川資，說是由我的自便；然而伊哭了，這正是情理中的事，因爲那時讀書應試是正路，所謂學洋務，社會上便以爲是一種走投無路的人，只得將靈魂賣給鬼子，要加倍的奚落而且排斥的，而況伊又看不見自己的兒子了。然而我也顧不得這些事，終于到N去進了K學堂了，在這學堂裏，我纔知道世上還有所謂格致、算學、地理、歷史、繪圖和體操。生理學並不敎，但我們卻看到些木版的《全體新論》和《化學衞生論》之類了。我還記得先前的醫生的議論和方藥，和現在所知道的比較起來，便漸漸的悟得中醫不過是一種有意的或無意的騙子，

然而	rán'ér	nevertheless
終于	zhōngyú	finally
日重一日	rì zhòng yí rì	to get more serious (worse) every day
亡故	wánggù	to die, to become deceased
小康人家	xiǎo kǎng rén jiā	a family by no means rich but in comfortable enough circumstances
墜入	zhuì rù	to fall into
困頓	kùndùn	straitened circumstances
塗路	túlù	path, way

N = Nanking

K 學堂	xuétáng = Kiangnan shǔishi xüétáng	The Kiangnan Naval School
彷彿	fǎngfú	it seems almost as if
尋求	xünqiú	to seek
沒有法	méiyǒu fǎ	to have no alternative but to
辦	bàn	to manage, to get together
川資	chuānzī	money for a journey, travelling expenses
自便	zìbiàn	to do as one pleases
伊	yī	but here used for 她 tā
情理中事	qínglǐ zhōng shǐ	only to be expected
應試	yìng shǐ	to sit for examination, more specifically, as here, for the traditional official examinations
正路	zhèng lù	proper path, orthodox path
洋務	yángwù	foreign things
走投無路	zǒu tóu wú lù	nowhere to turn to, at the end of one's tether
靈魂	línghún	soul
鬼子	guizi	devil – foreigner
奚落	xīluò	to deride, to jeer at
排斥	páichì	to exclude, to squeeze out
而況	érkuàng	what is more
顧不得	gù bù dé	no time to worry about or have scruples about
格致	gézhì	physics
算學	suànxüé	mathematics (more commonly today 數學 shù xüé)
繪圖	hùitú	drawing
體操	tǐcāo	physical training
生理學	shēnglǐ xüé	physiology
看到	kàn dào	to come across
木版	mùbǎn	wood block (for printing)
全體新論	quán tǐ xīn lùn	*New Treatise on the Human Body*
化學衛生論	huàxüé wèishēng lùn	*Treatise on Chemical Hygiene*
議論	yìlùn	views
方藥	fāngyào	prescriptions
比較	bǐjiào	to compare
悟	wù	to wake up to, to become aware of, to realise (for something to dawn on someone)
有意的	yǒuyì de	intentionally

同時又很起了對于被騙的病人和他的家族的同情；而且從譯出的歷史上，又知道了日本維新是大半發端于西方醫學的事實。

因為這些幼稚的知識，後來便使我的學籍列在日本一個鄉間的醫學專門學校裏了。我的夢很美滿，豫備卒業回來，救治像我父親似的被誤的病人的疾苦，戰爭時候便去當軍醫，一面又促進了國人對于維新的信仰。我已不知道教授微生物學的方法，現在又有了怎樣的進步了，總之那時是用了電影，來顯示微生物的形狀的，因此有時講義的一段落已完，而時間還沒有到，教師便映些風景或時事的畫片給學生看，以用去這多餘的光陰。其時正當日俄戰爭的時候，關于戰事的畫片自然也就比較的多了，我在這一個講堂中，便須常常隨喜我那同學們的拍手和喝采。有一回，我竟在畫片上忽然會見我久違的許多中國人了，一個綁在中間，許多站在左右，一樣是强壯的體格，而顯出麻木的神情。據解說，則綁着的是替俄國做了軍事上的偵探，正要被日軍砍下頭顱來示衆，而圍着的便是來賞鑑這示衆的盛舉的人們。

這一學年沒有完畢，我已經到了東京了，因為從那一回以後，我便覺得醫學並非一件緊要事，凡是愚弱的國民，即使體格如何健全，如何茁壯，也只能做

騙子	piànzi	swindler
家族	jiāzú	(members of the) family
同情	tóngqíng	sympathy
譯出	yì chū	translated
日本維新	rì běn wéixin	The Meiji Restoration (but wei xin more properly means "reforms")
發端	fā duān	to have the beginnings in, to originate
事實	shìshí	fact
幼稚	yòuzhì	puerile, rudimentary
學籍列在	xüéjí liè zài	to place one's name on the register of a school
美滿	měimǎn	perfect
豫備	yùbèi	all set to
卒業	zúyè	graduated
誤	wù	to miss or to cause to miss (opportunity); (here, of being cured)
促進	cùjìn	to promote
一面	yímiàn	at the same time
信仰	xìnyǎng	faith
微生物	wéishēng wù	microbes
顯示	xiǎnshì	to show up clearly
形狀	xíngzhuàng	shape, form
講義	jiǎngyì	lecture notes (but used here, rather in accordance with Japanese usage, to mean "lecture")
段落	duànluò	the end of a section, convenient point to stop
教師	jiàoshī	teacher
映	yìng	to project on screen
時事	shíshì	current events, news of the day
畫片	huàpiàn	pictures, slides
光陰	guāngyin	time (when the emphasis is on its value)
隨喜	suíxǐ	to join in the merriment (originally Buddhist)
喝采	hè cǎi	to cheer
久違	jiǔ wéi	not to have seen for a long time; (here sarc.)
綁	bǎng	to bind, to tie up; here to be tied up
站	zhàn	to stand
體格	tǐgé	physique
麻木	mámù	numbed
神情	shénqíng	expression (on face)
據解說	jù jiěshuō	according to the explanation (caption)
偵探	zhēntàn	detective, hence spy
砍下頭顱	kǎn xià tóulú	to be beheaded
示衆	shì zhòng	to be made a public example of
賞鑑	shǎngjiàn	to examine with appreciation (as in the case of a connoisseur examining a work of art) (here sarc.)
盛舉	shèng jǔ	magnificent event (here sarc.)
愚弱	yúruò	stupid and weak
健全	jiànquán	healthy, sound

毫無意義的示衆的材料和看客，病死多少是不必以爲
不幸的。所以我們的第一要著，是在改變他們的精神，
而善于改變精神的是，我那時以爲當然要推文藝，于
是想提倡文藝運動了。在東京的留學生很有學法政理
化以至警察工業的，但沒有人治文學和美術；可是在
冷淡的空氣中，也幸而尋到幾個同志了，此外又邀集
了必須的幾個人，商量之後，第一步當然是出雜誌，
名目是取『新的生命』的意思，因爲我們那時大抵帶
些復古的傾向，所以只謂之《新生》。

　　《新生》的出版之期接近了，但最先就隱去了若
干擔當文字的人，接着又逃走了資本，結果只剩下不
名一錢的三個人。創始時候旣已背時，失敗時候當然
無可告語，而其後卻連這三個人也都爲各自的運命所
驅策，不能在一處縱談將來的好夢了，這就是我們的
並未產生的《新生》的結局。

　　我感到未嘗經驗的無聊，是自此以後的事。我當

茁壯	zhuózhuàng	robust
毫無意義	háo wú yìyì	totally meaningless
看客	kànkè	spectator
病死	bìng sí	to die of illness
多少	duōshǎo	a certain number, a few
不幸	búxìng	unfortunate
著	zhuó	a move (in a chess game)
善于	shànyú	to be good at, for
推	tuī	to push up or to the front, hence to single out, to elect
提倡	tíchàng	to advocate, to champion (a cause)
運動	yùndòng	movement
法政理化	fǎ zhèng lǐ huà	law, politics, physics, chemistry
以至	yǐzhì	even as far as, (from) . . . to . . .
治	zhì	to go in for, to study (class.)
美術	měishù	fine art
冷淡	lěngdàn	cool, lukewarm, lacking in enthusiasm
同志	tóngzhì	kindred spirit, (later usage) comrade
邀集	yāojí	ask together
必須	bìxū	necessary
商量	shāngliáng	to discuss, discussion
名目	míngmù	title, name under which something is known
取⋯的意思	qǔ . . . de yìsi	chosen to give the sense of
大抵	dàdǐ	generally speaking
帶	dài	to show traces of, to smack of, tinged
復古	fù gǔ	revival of things ancient
傾向	qīngxiàng	tendency
出版	chūbǎn	to publish
期	qi	date
接近	jiējìn	to approach
隱去	yǐn qù	to disappear from sight
若干	ruògān	a certain number (or amount)
擔當	dāndāng	to undertake
接着	jiēzhe	immediately afterwards
逃走	táozǒu	to run away, to get off
資本	zīběn	capital
不名一錢	bù míng yì qián	without a cent to one's name, penniless
創始	chuàngshǐ	foundation, inauguration
背時	bèi shí	inopportune, inauspicious
無可告語	wú kě gàoyǔ	nowhere to turn to for a sympathetic hearing
運命	yùnmìng	fate
驅策	qūcè	to drive on, to goad
在一處	zài yí chù	to be together in the same place
縱談	zòng tán	to range freely in one's talk
並未產生	bìng wèi chǎn shēng	never brought forth in the world
結果	jiéguǒ	finale, hence how a thing ends, outcome
無聊	wúliáo	boredom, sense of futility; bored

初是不知其所以然的；後來想，凡有一人的主張，得了贊和，是促其前進的，得了反對，是促其奮鬥的，獨有叫喊于生人中，而生人並無反應，既非贊同，也無反對，如置身毫無邊際的荒原，無可措手的了，這是怎樣的悲哀呵，我于是以我所感到者爲寂寞。

這寂寞又一天一天的長大起來，如大毒蛇，纏住了我的靈魂了。

然而我雖然自有無端的悲哀，卻也並不憤懑，因爲這經驗使我反省，看見自己了：就是我決不是一個振臂一呼應者雲集的英雄。

只是我自己的寂寞是不可不驅除的，因爲這于我太痛苦。我于是用了種種法，來麻醉自己的靈魂，使我沈入于國民中，使我回到古代去，後來也親歷或旁觀過幾樣更寂寞、更悲哀的事，都爲我所不願追懷，甘心使他們和我的腦一同消滅在泥土裏的，但我的麻醉法卻也似乎已經奏了功，再沒有青年時候的慷慨激昂的意思了。

S 會館裏有三間屋，相傳是往昔曾在院子裏的槐樹上縊死過一個女人的，現在槐樹已經高不可攀了，而這屋還沒有人住；許多年，我便寓在這屋裏鈔古碑。

自此以後	zì cǐ yǐ hòu	henceforth
不知其所以然的	bù zhī qí sǔoyǐ rán de	not knowing why it is
主張	zhǔzhāng	what one advocates, to advocate
贊和	zànhè	to support
促	cù	to urge (forward)
奮鬪	fèndòu	to fight for, to struggle
叫喊	jiàohǎn	to shout
反應	fǎnyìng	reaction, to react
無邊際	wú biānjì	boundless
荒原	huāng yüán	wilderness
措手	cuòshǒu	way into a problem, to tackle
悲哀	bēiāi	sad
以 x 爲 y	yǐ x wéi y	to consider x to be y (class. construction)
毒蛇	dú shé	poisonous snake
纏住	chán zhu	to entwine
無端	wúduān	unaccountable
憤懣	fènmèn	bottled up anger
反省	fǎnxǐng	to reflect
決不是	jüé bú shì	definitely not
振臂一呼應者雲集	zhèn bèi yǐ hū yìng zhě yün jí	to be able to rally the multitude by simply raising a cry
驅除	qüchú	to rid, to drive out
麻醉	mázuì	to drug, to dope
沉入	chén rù	to sink into
親歷	qīn lì	to experience personally
旁觀	páng guān	to look on from the side
爲…所	wéi . . . sǔo	is what . . .
追懷	zhuīhuái	to recall
甘心	gānxīn	with no regrets, willingly (in spite of the possible consequences)
消滅	xiāomiè	to extinguish, to annihilate, to vanish
似乎	sì hū	to seem as if
奏功	zòu gōng	to be effective (class.)
慷慨激昂	kāng kǎi jí áng	heroic
S = Shàoxīng	紹興	
會館	huìguǎn	a club house (here for people who come from the same district)
屋	wū	building, house (the use of it for "room" is confined to the expression wūzi)
相傳	xiāngchuán	the story goes
往昔	wǎngxī	in the past
槐樹	huái shù	pagoda tree
縊	yì	to strangle, to hang
攀	pān	to reach up and either pull something down or oneself up
寓	yù	lodging, to lodge
鈔	chāo	to copy out by hand
古碑	gǔ bēi	ancient stone inscriptions

客中少有人來，古碑中也遇不到什麼問題和主義，而我的生命卻居然暗暗的消去了，這也就是我惟一的願望。夏夜，蚊子多了，便搖着蒲扇坐在槐樹下，從密葉縫裏看那一點一點的青天，晚出的槐蠶又每每冰冷的落在頭頸上。

那時偶或來談的是一個老朋友金心異，將手提的大皮夾放在破桌上，脫下長衫，對面坐下了，因為怕狗，似乎心房還在怦怦的跳動。

『你鈔了這些有什麼用？』有一夜，他翻着我那古碑的鈔本，發了研究的質問了。

『沒有什麼用。』

『那麼，你鈔他是什麼意思呢？』

『沒有什麼意思。』

『我想，你可以做點文章……』

我懂得他的意思了，他們正辦《新青年》，然而那時彷彿不特沒有人來贊同，並且也還沒有人來反對，我想，他們許是感到寂寞了，但是說：

『假如一間鐵屋子，是絕無窗戶而萬難破毀的，裏面有許多熟睡的人們，不久都要悶死了，然而是從昏睡入死滅，並不感到就死的悲哀。現在你大嚷起來，驚起了較為清醒的幾個人，使這不幸的少數者來受無可挽救的臨終的苦楚，你倒以為對得起他們麼？』

『然而幾個人既然起來，你不能說決沒有毀壞這鐵屋的希望。』

是的，我雖然自有我的確信，然而說到希望，卻

客中	kèzhōng	while living `as a *kè*, i.e. away from home or native place
居然	jūrán	actually, i.e., surprisingly (to be successful in)
暗暗的	ànàn de	quietly
消去	xiāoqù	to ebb away
願望	yüànwàng	wish, aspiration
從密葉縫裏	cóng mì yè fèng lǐ	from in between the dense foliage
蠶	cán	silk worm, also caterpillar
冰冷	bīnglěng	icy to the touch
偶或	ǒuhuò	very occasionally
手提的	shǒutí de	portable
皮夾	píjiā	brief case
破	pò	broken, battered
脫下	tuō xià	to take off
心房	xīnfáng	the heart (the physical organ)
翻	fān	to flip through
研究	yánjiū	research, probe
質問	zhì wèn	question, press for an answer, interrogate
辦	bàn	to run (a newspaper or magazine)
不特	bú tè = 不但	not only
絕無	jüé wú	jüe is an intensifier, hence not at all
破毀	pòhuǐ	to smash down
熟睡	shú shuì	sound asleep
悶死	mèn sǐ	to die of suffocation
昏睡	hūn shuì	drowsiness
死滅	sǐmiè	death and extinction (Buddhist flavour)
就死	jiù sǐ	about to die
大嚷	dà rǎng	to shout noisily
驚起	jīng qǐ	to arouse abruptly
清醒	qīng xǐng	in possession of one's senses
挽救	wǎnjiù	to save, to retrieve, to pull back from the brink to safety
臨終	línzhōng	the moment before death
苦楚	kǔchǔ	pain, agony
對得起	duì dé qǐ	to have done the right thing by someone
既然	jìrán	since
確信	qüèxìn	firm conviction

是不能抹殺的，因爲希望是在于將來，決不能以我之
必無的證明，來折服了他之所謂可有，于是我終于答
應他也做文章了，這便是最初的一篇《狂人日記》。
從此以後，便一發而不可收，每寫些小說模樣的文章
，以敷衍朋友們的囑託，積久就有了十餘篇。

　　在我自己，本以爲現在是已經並非一個切迫而不
能已于言的人了，但或者也還未能忘懷于當日自己的
寂寞的悲哀罷，所以有時候仍不免吶喊幾聲，聊以慰
藉那在寂寞裏奔馳的猛士，使他不憚于前驅。至于我
的喊聲是勇猛或是悲哀，是可憎或是可笑，那倒是不
暇顧及的；但旣然是吶喊，則當然須聽將令的了，所
以我往往不恤用了曲筆，在《藥》的瑜兒的墳上平空
添上一個花環，在《明天》裏也不敍單四嫂子竟沒有
做到看見兒子的夢，因爲那時的主將是不主張消極的。
至于自己，卻也並不願將自以爲苦的寂寞，再來傳染
給也如我那年青時候似的正做着好夢的青年。

　　這樣說來，我的小說和藝術的距離之遠，也就可

抹殺	mǒshā	to deny (unjustly the case for the other side), to suppress
在于	zài yú	to lie in
必無的證明	bì wú de zhèngmíng	proof that there cannot possibly be any (hope)
折服	zhéfú	to convince
所謂可有	suǒ wèi kě yǒu	what (he) calls possibly existent
答應	dāyìng	to agree to, to promise to
做文章	zuò wénzhāng	to write
一發而不可收	yǐ fā ér bù kě shōu	once started impossible to halt
每	měi	every now and then
模樣	móyàng	what looks like, (here "what passes for")
小說	xiǎoshuō	fiction
敷衍	fūyǎn	to do something perfunctory which does not fill the bill simply to be able to say that you have done your duty
囑託	zhǔtuō	what someone has solemnly asked you to do
積久	jī jiǔ	in the course of time
在我自己	zài wǒ zìjǐ	for my part
本以爲	běn yǐ wéi	(I) had thought
切迫而不能已于言	qièpò ér bù néng yǐ yü yán	to feel it so pressing as to be unable to desist from speaking
忘懷	wànghuái	to forget
仍不免	réng bù miǎn	still cannot help
聊以	liáo yǐ	merely to
慰藉	wèijiè	to comfort
奔馳	bēnchí	to rush around
猛士	měng shì	brave warriors
不憚	bú dàn	not afraid of, not to shrink from ready to brave
前驅	qián qū	to rush forward
可憎	kě zèng	detestable
不暇顧及	bú xià gù jí	no time to worry about
吶喊	nàhǎn	to raise a battle cry
須聽將令	xū tīng jiàng lìng	to have to listen to (obey) the orders of the commander
往往	wǎngwǎng	frequently
不恤	bù xù	to stoop to
曲筆	qū bǐ	distortion of the facts in one's writing
平(憑)空	píngkōng	totally fictitious, with no foundation at all
添上	tiān shàng	to add
花環	huāhuán	a wreath
敍	xü	to recount, to narrate
主將	zhǔjiàng	general-in-chief
不主張	bù zhǔzhāng	to be against
消極	xiāojí	negative, pessimist
傳染	chuánrǎn	to infect
這樣說來	zhèyàng shuō lái	looked at in this way

想而知了，然而到今日還能蒙着小說的名，甚而至于且有成集的機會，無論如何總不能不說是一件徼幸的事，但徼幸雖使我不安于心，而懸揣人間暫時還有讀者，則究竟也仍然是高興的。

所以我竟將我的短篇小說結集起來，而且付印了，又因爲上面所說的緣由，便稱之爲《吶喊》。

距離	jùlí	the distance between
可想而知	kě xiǎng ér zhī	can be imagined
蒙着…的名	méngzhe . . . de míng	to pass off as
成集	chéng jí	to be collected into a volume
無論如何	wú lùn rú hé	however you look at it
徼幸	jiǎo xìng	lucky
不安于心	bù ān yǔ xīn	uneasy in one's mind
懸揣	xüánchuǎi	to conjecture
暫時	zànshí	for the moment
短篇小說	duǎn piān xiǎoshuō	short stories
結集起來	jiéjí qi lái	to collect together
付印	fù yìn	to give to the printer
緣由	yüanyóu	how a thing comes about

狂人日記

　　某君昆仲，今隱其名，皆余昔日在中學校時良友；分隔多年，消息漸闕。日前偶聞其一大病；適歸故鄉，迂道往訪，則僅晤一人，言病者其弟也。勞君遠道來視，然已早愈，赴某地候補矣。因大笑，出示日記二册，謂可見當日病狀，不妨獻諸舊友。持歸閱一過，知所患蓋『迫害狂』之類。語頗錯雜無倫次，又多荒唐之言；亦不著月日，惟墨色字體不一，知非一時所書。間亦有略具聯絡者，今撮錄一篇，以供醫家研究，記中語誤，一字不易；惟人名雖皆村人，不為世間所知，無關大體，然亦悉易去。至于書名，則本人愈後

狂人日記　Kuáng rén rìjì

某君	mǒu jūn	Mr. X
昆仲	kūnzhòng	brothers
隱	yǐn	to leave anonymous
余	yú	I
艮友	liáng yǒu	good friends
消息	xiāoxi	news
漸	jiàn	gradually
闕（＝缺）	qüē	lacking
日前	rìqián	the other day
適	shì	happening
迂道	yū dào	to make a detour
往	wǎng	to go to
僅	jǐn	only
晤	wù	to meet
勞	láo	it is good of you to have taken the trouble to
視	shì	to visit; to see how one is
愈	yù	recovered
候補	hòu bǔ	having the qualifications but waiting for a vacancy
示	shì	to show
日記	rìjì	diary
當日	dāngrì	at that time
病狀	bìngzhuàng	the symptoms of his illness
不妨	bùfáng	no harm in
獻	xiàn	to present to
諸（＝之於）	zhū	it (them) to
閱	yüè	to look over
患	huàn	to suffer from
迫害狂	pòhài kuáng	persecution mania
語	yǔ	words, speech
錯雜	cuòzá	mixed up
無論次	wú lúncì	disordered
荒唐	huāngtáng	wild, preposterous
著	zhuó	to attach
間	jiàn	occasionally, here and there
具	jù	to be possessed of
聯絡	liánluò	connection
撮錄	cuò lù	to abstract, to give an extract
供	gōng	to furnish
語誤	yǔwù	slip of the pen (or tongue)
易	yì	to change
無關大體	wú guān dàtǐ	of no great consequence

所題，不復改也。七年四月二日識。

一

　　今天晚上，很好的月光。

　　我不見他，已是三十多年；今天見了，精神分外
爽快。纔知道以前的三十多年，全是發昏；然而須十
分小心。不然，那趙家的狗，何以看我兩眼呢？

　　我怕得有理。

二

　　今天全沒月光，我知道不妙。早上小心出門，趙
貴翁的眼色便怪：似乎怕我，似乎想害我。還有七八
個人，交頭接耳的議論我。又怕我看見。一路上的人，
都是如此。其中最凶的一個人，張着嘴，對我笑了一
笑；我便從頭直冷到脚跟，曉得他們布置，都已妥當
了。

　　我可不怕，仍舊走我的路。前面一夥小孩子，也
在那里議論我；眼色也同趙貴翁一樣，臉色也都鐵青。
我想我同小孩子有什麼讎，他也這樣。忍不住大聲說，
『你告訴我！』他們可就跑了。

　　我想：我同趙貴翁有什麼讎，同路上的人又有什
麼讎；只有廿年以前，把古久先生的陳年流水簿子，
踹了一脚，古久先生很不高興。趙貴翁雖然不認識他，
一定也聽到風聲，代抱不平；約定路上的人，同我作
冤對。但是小孩子呢？那時候，他們還沒有出世，何
以今天也睜着怪眼睛，似乎怕我，似乎想害我。這眞
教我怕，教我納罕而且傷心。

　　我明白了。這是他們娘老子教的！

悉	xī	completely
題	tí	to entitle
識	zhì	to make a note
爽快	shuǎngkuài	refreshed
發昏	fāhūn	in a daze
不妙	búmiào	something is wrong, it bodes ill
眼色	yǎnsè	look in the eyes
交頭接耳	jiāo tóu jiē ěr	whispering with their heads together
議論	yìlùn	to discuss
脚跟	jiǎogēn	heels
布置	bùzhì	arrangements, laying of a trap
妥當	tuǒdàng	in place
鐵青	tiěqīng	livid
讎	chóu	enmity
廿	niàn	twenty
陳年	chénnián	over many many years; (of wine) vintage
流水簿子	liúshuǐ bùzǐ	account book, journal
踹	chuài	to tread on
風聲	fēngshēng	rumour, (to get) wind (of)
代	dài	on someone's behalf
抱不平	bào bùpíng	to stand up for another, take up cudgels (on someone's behalf)
約定	yuē dìng	made an arrangement beforehand with
作寃對	zuò yuānduì	to be implacably against someone
納罕	nàhǎn	to wonder
娘老子	niánglǎozǐ	mother and father

三

晚上總是睡不着。凡事須得研究，纔會明白。

他們——也有給知縣打枷過的，也有給紳士掌過嘴的，也有衙役佔了他妻子的，也有老子娘被債主逼死的；他們那時候的臉色，全沒有昨天這麼怕，也沒有這麼凶。

最奇怪的是昨天街上的那個女人，打他兒子，嘴裏說道，『老子呀！我要咬你幾口纔出氣！』他眼睛卻看着我。我出了一驚，遮掩不住；那青面獠牙的一夥人，便都哄笑起來。陳老五趕上前，硬把我拖回家中了。

拖我回家。家裏的人都裝作不認識我；他們的眼色，也全同別人一樣。進了書房，便反扣上門，宛然是關了一隻雞鴨。這一件事，越教我猜不出底細。

前幾天，狼子村的佃戶來告荒，對我大哥說，他們村裏的一個大惡人，給大家打死了；幾個人便挖出他的心肝來，用油煎炒了喫，可以壯壯膽子。我插了一句嘴，佃戶和大哥便都看我幾眼。今天纔曉得他們的眼光，全同外面的那夥人一模一樣。

想起來，我從頂上直冷到脚跟。

他們會喫人，就未必不會喫我。

你看那女人『咬你幾口』的話，和一夥青面獠牙人的笑，和前天佃戶的話，明明是暗號。我看出他話中全是毒，笑中全是刀，他們的牙齒，全是白厲厲的排着，這就是喫人的傢伙。

枷	jiā	cangue
掌嘴	zhǎng zuǐ	to smack the mouth
衙役	yáyì	yamen runners
佔	zhàn	to take over what belongs to another by force
逼死	bī sǐ	to drive to death through persecution
出了一驚	chū le yì jīng	to give a start
遮掩	zhēyǎn	to cover up
獠牙	liáoyá	fanged teeth
裝作	zhuāngzuò	to pretend to
反扣上門	fǎn kòu shàng mén	to latch the door from the outside
宛然	wǎnrán	just as if
越	yüè	all the more
猜	cāi	to guess
底細	dǐxì	what was behind it, low-down
佃戶	diànhù	tenant farmer
告荒	gào huāng	to report a famine
挖出	wā chū	to gouge out
煎炒	jiānchǎo	to fry
壯膽	zhuàng dǎn	to bolster up one's courage
插嘴	chā zuǐ	to interrupt, to put a word in
暗號	ànhào	signal
白厲厲	báilìlì	[?] frighteningly white
傢伙	jiāhuǒ	tools, gear

照我自己想，雖然不是惡人，自從踹了古家的簿子，可就難說了。他們似乎別有心思，我全猜不出。況且他們一翻臉，便說人是惡人。我還記得大哥教我做論，無論怎樣好人，翻他幾句，他便打上幾個圈；原諒壞人幾句，他便說『翻天妙手，與衆不同。』我那里猜得到他們的心思，究竟怎樣；況且是要喫的時候。

凡事總須研究，纔會明白。古來時常喫人，我也還記得，可是不甚清楚。我翻開歷史一查，這歷史沒有年代，歪歪斜斜的每葉上都寫着『仁義道德』幾個字。我橫豎睡不着，仔細看了半夜，纔從字縫裏看出字來，滿本都寫着兩個字是『喫人』！

書上寫着這許多字，佃戶說了這許多話，卻都笑吟吟的睜着怪眼睛看我。

我也是人，他們想要喫我了！

四

早上，我靜坐了一會。陳老五送進飯來，一碗菜，一碗蒸魚；這魚的眼睛，白而且硬，張着嘴，同那一夥想喫人的人一樣。喫了幾筷，滑溜溜的不知是魚是人，便把他兜肚連腸的吐出。

我說『老五，對大哥說，我悶得慌，想到園裏走走。』老五不答應，走了，停一會，可就來開了門。

我也不動，研究他們如何擺佈我；知道他們一定不肯放鬆。果然！我大哥引了一個老頭子，慢慢走來；他滿眼凶光，怕我看出，只是低頭向着地，從眼鏡橫

照我自己想	zhào wǒ zìjǐ xiǎng	the way I look at it
別有心思	bié yǒu xīnsī	to have their own way of looking at things
翻臉	fānliǎn	to turn nasty
做論	zuò lùn	to write essays
翻	fān	to reverse the verdict
打圈	dǎ quān	to mark the best passages with circles beside the characters
原諒	yüánliàng	to excuse
翻天妙手與衆不同	fān tiān miào shǒu yǚ zhòng bù tóng	the skill which turns the heavens up-side down and quite different from the run of the mill
古來	gǔlái	down the ages
翻開	fān kāi	to open (book)
查	chá	to look up (dictionary, reference book)
年代	niándài	dates
歪歪斜斜	wāi wāi xié xié	in wobbly lines
橫豎	héngshù	in any case, anyway
字縫裏	zìfèng lǐ	in between the lines
笑吟吟	xiào yín yín	with a smiling face
靜坐	jìng zuò	to sit quietly, to sit as in meditation
蒸	zhēng	to steam (food)
硬	yìng	hard
張	zhāng	to open
幾筷	jǐ kuài	several chopstickfuls
滑溜溜	huá liū liū	slippery, slimy
兜肚連腸	dōu dù lián cháng	stomachs, intestines and all
悶得慌	mèn dé huāng	I feel awful being cooped up
走走	zǒu zǒu	to take a walk
答應	dāyìng	to reply; to agree to a request
擺佈	bǎibù	to manipulate, to do with
放鬆	fàngsōng	to let up
凶光	xiōng guāng	ferocious gleam
看出	kàn chū	to make out

邊暗暗看我。大哥說，『今天你彷彿很好。』我說
『是的。』大哥說，『今天請何先生來，給你診一診。』
我說『可以！』其實我豈不知道這老頭子是劊子手扮
的！無非借了看脈這名目，揣一揣肥瘠。因這功勞，
也分一片肉喫。我也不怕；雖然不喫人，膽子卻比他
們還壯。伸出兩個拳頭，看他如何下手。老頭子坐着，
閉了眼睛，摸了好一會，呆了好一會；便張開他鬼眼
睛說，『不要亂想。靜靜的養幾天，就好了。』

　　不要亂想，靜靜的養！養肥了，他們是自然可以
多喫；我有什麼好處，怎麼會『好了』？他們這羣人，
又想喫人，又是鬼鬼祟祟，想法子遮掩，不敢直捷下
手，真要令我笑死。我忍不住，便放聲大笑起來，十
分快活。自己曉得這笑聲裏面，有的是義勇和正氣。
老頭子和大哥，都失了色，被我這勇氣正氣鎮壓住了。

　　但是我有勇氣，他們便越想喫我，沾光一點這勇
氣。老頭子跨出門，走不多遠，便低聲對大哥說道，
『趕緊喫罷！』大哥點點頭。原來也有你！這一件大
發見，雖似意外，也在意中：合夥喫我的人，便是我
的哥哥！

　　喫人的是我哥哥！

　　我是喫人的人的兄弟！

　　我自己被人喫了，可仍然是喫人的人的兄弟！

五

　　這幾天是退一步想：假使那老頭子不是劊子手扮
的，真是醫生，也仍然是喫人的人。他們的祖師李時

劊子手	kuàizishǒu	the executioner
扮	bàn	to assume the guise of, to play the part of
看脈	kànmò	to examine the pulse, to examine a patient
揣	chuǎi	to weigh up
肥瘠	féijí	(class.) fat and thin, degree of fatness
功勞	gōngláo	service
分	fēn	to have a share
下手	xià shǒu	to set about doing something (often nasty)
閉	bì	to shut
摸	mō	to feel (with one's hand)
呆	dāi	to be lost in thought
鬼	guǐ	evil
亂想	luàn xiǎng	to have uncontrolled thoughts
養	yǎng	to rest
鬼鬼祟祟	guǐ guǐ suì suì	furtive, surreptitious, sneaky
遮掩	zhēyǎn	to cover up
直捷	zhíjié	without beating about the bush
義勇	yìyǒng	righteous courage
正氣	zhèngqì	moral force that permeates the universe
失了色	shī le sè	turned pale
鎮壓	zhènyā	to keep down (by superior weight or authority), to dominate
沾光	zhān guāng	to derive some benefit from someone else's prestige, achievement or generosity
趕緊喫	gǎn jǐn chī	must be eaten immediately. No time should be lost
原來也有你	yüán lái yě yǒu nǐ	Is that how it was? You were in it all along
發見(現)	fāxiàn	discovery
意中	yìzhōng	to be expected (ant. 意外)
退一步想	tuǐ yǐ bù xiǎng	to grant that things may not be as bad as one thought
假使	jiǎshǐ	suppose
祖師	zǔshi	the founder of a school, sect, etc.

珍做的『本草什麼』上，明明寫着人肉可以煎喫；他
還能說自己不喫人麼？

　　至于我家大哥，也毫不寃枉他。他對我講書的時
候，親口說過可以『易子而食』；又一回偶然議論起
一個不好的人，他便說不但該殺，還當『食肉寢皮』。
我那時年紀還小，心跳了好半天。前天狼子村佃戶來
說喫心肝的事，他也毫不奇怪，不住的點頭。可見心
思是同從前一樣狠。旣然可以『易子而食』，便什麼
都易得，什麼人都喫得。我從前單聽他講道理，也胡
塗過去；現在曉得他講道理的時候，不但唇邊還抹着
人油，而且心裏滿裝着喫人的意思。

<h2 style="text-align:center">六</h2>

　　黑漆漆的，不知是日是夜。趙家的狗又叫起來了。

　　獅子似的凶心，兔子的怯弱，狐狸的狡猾，……

<h2 style="text-align:center">七</h2>

　　我曉得他們的方法，直捷殺了，是不肯的，而且
也不敢，怕有禍祟。所以他們大家連絡，布滿了羅網，
逼我自戕。試看前幾天街上男女的樣子，和這幾天我
大哥的作爲，便足可悟出八九分了。最好是解下腰帶，
掛在梁上，自己緊緊勒死；他們沒有殺人的罪名，又
償了心願，自然都歡天喜地的發出一種嗚嗚咽咽的笑
聲。否則驚嚇憂愁死了，雖則略瘦，也還可以首肯幾
下。

　　他們是只會喫死肉的！——記得什麼書上說，有
一種東西，叫『海乙那』的，眼光和樣子都很難看；

本草什麼	běncǎo shénme	ben cao something [The Speaker has forgotten the rest of the title of the book] (*Ben Cao* is the encyclopaedia of herbal medicine)
煎	jiān	to boil (medicine)
冤枉	yuānwǎng	to accuse an innocent person
易子而食	yì zǐ ér shí	to exchange their sons for food (allusion comes from *Zuo Zhuan* 左傳 Duke Ai 8)
食肉寢皮	shí ròu qǐn pí	to eat his flesh and use his skin for a rug to sleep on (*Zuo Zhuan* Duke Hsiang 21)
點頭	diǎn tóu	to nod in approval
狠	hěn	cruel
胡塗過去	hútú guò qù	to muddle through
抹着	mò zhe	smeared with
滿裝	mǎn zhuāng	filled with
黑漆漆	hēi qīqī	pitch dark
怯弱	qièruò	cowardice, timidity
狡猾	jiǎohuá	cunning
直捷	zhíjié	outright
禍祟	huòsuì	disaster brought on by spirits
連絡	liánluò	to establish connection with
布羅網	bù luówǎng	to spread out nets
逼	bī	to force
自戕	zì qiáng	to kill oneself
作爲	zuòwéi	the doings
悟出	wù chū	to hit on (the solution), to figure out
腰帶	yāodài	belt
掛	guà	to hang from
梁	liáng	beam
緊緊	jǐnjǐn	tightly
勒	lè	to tighten a cord
勒死	lè sǐ	to strangle with a cord
償心願	chǎng xīnyuàn	to gratify one's long-felt desire
歡天喜地	huān tiān xǐ dì	with rejoicing
否則	fǒuzé	failing that; otherwise
驚嚇憂愁	jīngxià yōuchóu	through fright and grief
首肯	shǒukěn	to nod in approval or assent
海乙那	hǎiyìná	hyena

時常喫死肉，連極大的骨頭，都細細嚼爛，嚥下肚子去，想起來也敎人害怕。『海乙那』是狼的親眷，狼是狗的本家。前天趙家的狗，看我幾眼，可見他也同謀，早已接洽。老頭子眼看着地。豈能瞞得我過。

最可憐的是我的大哥，他也是人，何以毫不害怕；而且合夥喫我呢？還是歷來慣了，不以爲非呢？還是喪了良心，明知故犯呢？

我詛咒喫人的人，先從他起頭；要勸轉喫人的人，也先從他下手。

八

其實這種道理，到了現在，他們也該早已懂得，……

忽然來了一個人；年紀不過二十左右，相貌是不很看得清楚，滿面笑容，對了我點頭，他的笑也不像眞笑。我便問他，『喫人的事，對麼？』他仍然笑着說，『不是荒年，怎麼會喫人。』我立刻就曉得，他也是一夥，喜歡喫人的；便自勇氣百倍，偏要問他。

『對麼？』

『這等事問他甚麼。你眞會……說笑話。……今天天氣很好。』

天氣是好，月色也很亮了。可是我要問你，『對麼？』

他不以爲然了。含含胡胡的答道，『不……』

『不對？他們何以竟喫?!』

『沒有的事……』

骨頭	gǔtóu	bones
嚼爛	jiǎo làn	to chew to a pulp
嚥	yān	to swallow
親眷	qīnjüàn	relations (by marriage)
同謀	tóngmóu	in it together, accomplice
接洽	jiēqiá	to negotiate
歷來	lìlái	all along, always
慣	guàn	to get used to
喪了良心	sàng le liángxīn	lost his conscience
明知故犯	míng zhǐ gù fàn	to transgress knowing full well that it is wrong
詛咒	zǔzhòu	to curse
勸轉	qüàn zhuǎn	to dissuade
相貌	xiàngmào	appearance, facial features
對	duì	right
仍然	réngrán	to go on as before
荒年	huāngnián	year of famine
立刻	lìkè	at once
百倍	bǎi bèı	a hundredfold
這等事	zhè děng shǐ	such things
不以為然	bù yǐ wéi rán	to disapprove

　　『沒有的事？狼子村現喫；還有書上都寫着，通紅嶄新！』

　　他便變了臉，鐵一般青。睜着眼說，『也許有的，這是從來如此……』

　　『從來如此，便對麼？』

　　『我不同你講這些道理；總之你不該說，你說便是你錯！』

　　我直跳起來，張開眼，這人便不見了。全身出了一大片汗。他的年紀，比我大哥小得遠，居然也是一夥；這一定是他娘老子先教的。還怕已經教給他兒子了；所以連小孩子，也都惡狠狠的看我。

<h2 style="text-align:center">九</h2>

　　自己想喫人，又怕被別人喫了，都用着疑心極深的眼光，面面相覷。……

　　去了這心思，放心做事走路喫飯睡覺，何等舒服。這只是一條門檻，一個關頭。他們可是父子、兄弟、夫婦、朋友、師生、仇敵和各不相識的人，都結成一夥，互相勸勉，互相牽掣，死也不肯跨過這一步。

<h2 style="text-align:center">十</h2>

　　大清早，去尋我大哥；他立在堂門外看天，我便走到他背後，攔住門，格外沈靜，格外和氣的對他說，

　　『大哥，我有話告訴你。』

　　『你說就是，』他趕緊回過臉來，點點頭。

　　『我只有幾句話，可是說不出來。大哥，大約當初野蠻的人，都喫過一點人。後來因為心思不同，有

通紅嶄新	tōng hóng zhǎn xīn	bright red and brand new
也許	yěxǔ	perhaps
從來如此	cónglái rúzǐ	it has always been the case
疑心	yíxin	suspicion
極深	jí shēn	exceedingly deep
面面相覷	miàn miàn xiāng qù	to look at one another not knowing what to do
心思	xīnsī	thoughts
門檻	ménkǎn	door sill
關頭	guāntóu	obstacle, crisis
師生	shī shēng	teacher and pupil
仇敵	chóudí	enemies
各不相識的人	gè bù xiāng shì de rén	strangers
互相勸勉	hù xiāng qüànmiǎn	to encourage one another
互相牽掣（制）	hù xiāng qiānzhì	to hinder one another
死也不	sǐ yě bù	simply would not
攔住	lán zhù	to bar the way
你說就是	nǐ shuō jiùshì	go ahead
野蠻	yěmán	uncivilised, savage, barbarous

的不喫人了，一味要好，便變了人，變了眞的人。有的卻還喫，——也同蟲子一樣，有的變了魚、鳥、猴子，一直變到人。有的不要好，至今還是蟲子。這喫人的人比不喫人的人，何等慚愧。怕比蟲子的慚愧猴子，還差得很遠很遠。

　　易牙蒸了他兒子，給桀紂喫，還是一直從前的事。**誰曉得從盤古開闢天地以後，一直喫到易牙的兒子；從易牙的兒子，一直喫到徐錫林**；從徐錫林，又一直喫到狠子村捉住的人。去年城裏殺了犯人，還有一個生癆病的人，用饅頭蘸血舐。

　　他們要喫我，你一個人，原也無法可想；然而又何必去入夥。喫人的人，什麼事做不出；他們會喫我，也會喫你，一夥裏面，也會自喫。但只要轉一步，只要立刻改了，也就人人太平。雖然從來如此，我們今天也可以格外要好，說是不能！大哥，我相信你能說，前天佃戶要減租，你說過不能。』

　　當初，他還只是冷笑，隨後眼光便凶狠起來，一到說破他們的隱情，那就滿臉都變成靑色了。大門外立着一夥人，趙貴翁和他的狗，也在裏面，都探頭探腦的挨進來。有的是看不出面貌，似乎用布蒙着；有的是仍舊靑面獠牙，抿着嘴笑。我認識他們是一夥，都是喫人的人。可是也曉得他們心思很不一樣，一種是以爲從來如此，應該喫的；一種是知道不該喫，可是仍然要喫，又怕別人說破他，所以聽了我的話，越發氣憤不過，可是抿着嘴冷笑。

一味	yíwèi	unswervingly
要好	yào hǎo	to want to be good
真的	zhēnde	real, genuine
猴子	hóuzǐ	monkey
慚愧	cánkuì	ashamed
桀紂	jié zhòu	tyrants who have become byword for wickedness
一直從前	yìzhí cóngqián	way back
盤古	pángǔ	legendary king who separated heaven and earth
徐錫林(麟)	Xú Xī Lín	revolutionary executed after he assassinated En-ming, the governor of An Hui in 1907. En-ming's guards gouged out his heart and ate it
癆病	láo bìng	consumption
蘸	zhàn	to dip into
無法可想	wú fǎ kě xiǎng	nothing can be done
什麼事做不出	shénmě shì zuò bù chū	what will they stop at
人人太平	rén rén tàipíng	everyone will be safe
冷笑	lěngxiào	smile coldly
凶狠	xiōnghěn	fierce
說破隱情	shūo pò yǐnqíng	to reveal their secrets, to bring into the open
探頭探腦	tàn tóu tàn nǎo	poking their heads in
挨進來	āi jǐn lái	to slink in
蒙着	méng zhe	covered up with cloth
抿着嘴	mǐn zhe zuǐ	to purse one's lips
越發	yüèfā	all the more
氣憤不過	qì fèn bú guò	most angry

　　這時候，大哥也忽然顯出凶相，高聲喝道，

　　『都出去！瘋子有什麼好看！』

　　這時候，我又懂得一件他們的巧妙了。他們豈但不肯改，而且早已布置；豫備下一個瘋子的名目罩上我。將來喫了，不但太平無事，怕還會有人見情。佃戶說的大家喫了一個惡人，正是這方法。這是他們的老譜！

　　陳老五也氣憤憤的直走進來。如何按得住我的口，我偏要對這夥人說，

　　『你們可以改了，從眞心改起！要曉得將來容不得喫人的人，活在世上。

　　你們要不改，自己也會喫盡。即使生得多，也會給眞的人除滅了，同獵人打完狼子一樣！——同蟲子一樣！』

　　那一夥人，都被陳老五趕走了。大哥也不知那里去了。陳老五勸我回屋子裏去。屋裏面全是黑沈沈的。橫梁和椽子都在頭上發抖；抖了一會，就大起來，堆在我身上。

　　萬分沈重，動彈不得；他的意思是要我死。我曉得他的沈重是假的，便掙扎出來，出了一身汗。可是偏要說，

　　『你們立刻改了，從眞心改起！你們要曉得將來是容不得喫人的人，……』

十一

　　太陽也不出，門也不開，日日是兩頓飯。

顯出兇相	xiǎn chū xiōng xiàng	to reveal his true ferocious appearance
喝	hè	to shout
瘋子	fēngzǐ	madman
巧妙	qiǎomiào	cunning trick
布置	bùzhǐ	to lay plans
豫備下	yùbèi xià	to have ready
名目	míngmù	label
罩上	zhào shàng	to put over (like a hood)
見情	jiànqíng	to sympathise, to excuse
老譜	lǎo pǔ	old formula
按住	àn zhù	to press down
按住我的口	àn zhù wǒ de kǒu	to put a hand over my mouth
眞心	zhēnxǐn	true heart, bottom of the heart
容	róng	to tolerate
除滅	chúmiè	to exterminate
椽子	chuánzǐ	rafters
萬分	wànfēn	extremely, exceedingly
動彈	dòngtan	to move (parts of the body)
掙扎	zhēngzhá	to struggle, to wriggle

我捏起筷子，便想起我大哥；曉得妹子死掉的緣故，也全在他。那時我妹子纔五歲，可愛可憐的樣子，還在眼前。母親哭個不住，他卻勸母親不要哭；大約因爲自己喫了，哭起來不免有點過意不去。如果還能過意不去，……

妹子是被大哥喫了，母親知道沒有，我可不得而知。

母親想也知道；不過哭的時候，卻並沒有說明，大約也以爲應當的了。記得我四五歲時，坐在堂前乘涼，大哥說爺娘生病，做兒子的須割下一片肉來，煮熟了請他喫，纔算好人；母親也沒有說不行。一片喫得，整個的自然也喫得。但是那天的哭法，現在想起來，實在還教人傷心，這眞是奇極的事！

十二

不能想了。

四千年來時時喫人的地方，今天纔明白，我也在其中混了多年；大哥正管着家務，妹子恰恰死了，他未必不和在飯菜裏，暗暗給我們喫。

我未必無意之中，不喫了我妹子的幾片肉，現在也輪到我自己，……

有了四千年喫人履歷的我，當初雖然不知道，現在明白，難見眞的人！

十三

沒有喫過人的孩子，或者還有？

救救孩子……

捏	niè	to grasp
過意不去	guò yì bú qù	to feel ill at ease, to feel sorry
說明	shuōmíng	to say so plainly
乘涼	chéngliáng	to enjoy the cool air
爺娘	yéniáng	father and mother
整個	zhěnggè	a whole
混	hùn	to get by, to live
家務	jiāwù	running of the family
和	hé	to mix in
無意之中	wú yì zhī zhōng	unwittingly
履歷	lǚlì	history, curriculum vitae
難見	nán jiàn	difficult to face

孔乙己

　　魯鎮的酒店的格局，是和別處不同的：都是當街一個曲尺形的大櫃臺，櫃裏面豫備着熱水，可以隨時溫酒。做工的人，傍午傍晚散了工，每每花四文銅錢，買一碗酒，——這是二十多年前的事，現在每碗要漲到十文，——靠櫃外站着，熱熱的喝了休息；倘肯多花一文，便可以買一碟鹽煮筍，或者茴香豆，做下酒物了，如果出到十幾文，那就能買一樣葷菜，但這些顧客，多是短衣幫，大抵沒有這樣闊綽。只有穿長衫的，纔踱進店面隔壁的房子裏，要酒要菜，慢慢地坐喝。

　　我從十二歲起，便在鎮口的咸亨酒店裏當夥計，掌櫃說，樣子太傻，怕侍候不了長衫主顧，就在外面做點事罷。外面的短衣主顧，雖然容易說話，但嘮嘮叨叨纏夾不清的也很不少。他們往往要親眼看着黃酒從罈子裏舀出，看過壺子底裏有水沒有，又親看將壺子放在熱水裏，然後放心：在這嚴重監督之下，羼水也很爲難。所以過了幾天，掌櫃又說我幹不了這事。幸虧薦頭的情面大，辭退不得，便改爲專管溫酒的一

孔乙己　Kǒng Yǐ Jǐ

魯鎮	Lǔ zhèn	A fictitious place name. Lu Xün chose it because Lu was the name of his mother's family
格局	géjú	layout
當街	dāng jiē	facing the street, up against the street
曲尺	qūchǐ	carpenter's square, right-angled shape
隨時	suíshí	any time
傍	bàng	(pref.) towards
漲	zhàng	to rise (water level, prices)
靠	kào	close up to
熱熱的	rè rè de	while it is hot
筍（笋）	sǔn	bamboo shoots
茴香豆	huíxiāng dòu	aniseed flavoured boiled broad beans
下	xià	to go with (rice or wine)
下酒	xià jiǔ	(food) to go with the wine
葷菜	hūn cài	meat dish, non-vegetarian dish
顧客	gùkè	customers
幫	bāng	gang, fraternity
闊綽	kuòchuò	liberal (in spending)
踱	duò	to walk in measured steps
隔壁	gébì	next door
口	kǒu	(suff.) entrance to
咸亨	xiánhēng	咸 is the name of the 31st hexagram in the *Book of Changes*. The text to this hexagram begins with the words 咸亨．亨 means "unimpeded" hence successful, prosperous. As xian can mean "all", xian heng means "prosperity all round", a very suitable name for a wine shop. Incidentally, this is the name of a real wineshop of the time.
掌櫃	zhǎngguì	manager
傻	shǎ	idiotic
不了	bù liǎo	(verb. suffix) unable to cope
侍候	shì hòu	wait on, attend to
嘮嘮叨叨	láoláo dāodāo	to go on and on about something
纏夾不清	chánjiā bù qīng	getting things all mixed up
罈子	tánzǐ	jar
舀	yǎo	to ladle out
嚴重	yánzhòng	strict, serious
監督	jiāndū	supervision
羼	chàn	to mix in, to adulterate
薦頭	jiàntóu	sponsor, one who recommends another for a job

種無聊職務了。

　　我從此便整天的站在櫃臺裏，專管我的職務。雖然沒有什麼失職，但總覺有些單調，有些無聊。掌櫃是一副凶臉孔，主顧也沒有好聲氣，教人活潑不得；只有孔乙己到店，纔可以笑幾聲，所以至今還記得。

　　孔乙己是站着喝酒而穿長衫的唯一的人。他身材很高大；青白臉色，皺紋間時常夾些傷痕；一部亂蓬蓬的花白的鬍子。穿的雖然是長衫，可是又髒又破，似乎十多年沒有補，也沒有洗。他對人說話，總是滿口之乎者也，教人半懂不懂的。因爲他姓孔，別人便從描紅紙上的『上大人孔乙己』這半懂不懂的話裏，替他取下一個綽號，叫作孔乙己。孔乙己一到店，所有喝酒的人便都看着他笑，有的叫道，『孔乙己，你臉上又添上新傷疤了！』他不回答，對櫃裏說，『溫兩碗酒，要一碟茴香豆。』便排出九文大錢。他們又故意的高聲嚷道，『你一定又偷了人家的東西了！』孔乙己睜大眼睛說，『你怎麼這樣憑空汚人清白……』『什麼清白？我前天親眼見你偷了何家的書，弔着打。』孔乙己便漲紅了臉，額上的青筋條條綻出，爭辯道，『竊書不能算偷……竊書！……讀書人的事，能算偷麼？』接連便是難懂的話，什麼『君子固窮』，什麼『者乎』之類，引得衆人都哄笑起來；店內外充滿了快活的空氣。

　　聽人家背地裏談論，孔乙己原來也讀過書，但終于沒有進學，又不會營生；于是愈過愈窮，弄到將要

情面	qíngmiàn	weight or prestige (of the sponsor)
辭退	cítuì	to give the sack
專管	zhuān guǎn	to be in charge solely of, with duties limited to . . . only
失職	shī zhí	to fail in one's duties
總覺	zǒng jüé	cannot help feeling
單調	dāndiào	monotonous
副	fù	(measure word) a set of
沒有好聲氣	méi yǒu hǎo shēng qì	never in civil tones
活潑	huópō	lively
青白	qīngbái	(of complexion) pale, pallid
皺紋	zhòuwén	wrinkles
夾着	jiā zhe	mixed with, sandwiched with, interspersed with
傷痕	shānghén	marks of injury
亂蓬蓬	luànpéngpéng	dishevelled
花白	huābái	grey streaked with white
滿口	mǎnkǒu	full of (in speech)
之乎者也	zhī hū zhě yě	classical particles, hence speech peppered with classical expressions and constructions
半懂不懂	bàn dǒng bù dǒng	half intelligible
描紅紙	miáohóng zhǐ	copy book with characters in red for children to trace over with black ink
上大人孔乙己		the characters on the opening page of the copybook
綽號	chuòhào	nickname
傷疤	shāngbā	scar, scab
排	pái	to lay out in a row
故意	gùyì	deliberately
你一定……	nǐ yī dìng . . .	it must be that you . . .
汙	wū	to blemish
清白	qīngbái	unsullied reputation
弔着打	diào zhe dǎ	to beat someone, having strung him up first
漲紅了臉	zhàng hóng le liǎn	to blush all over one's face (漲 puffed up)
青筋	qīngjīn	veins
綻出	zhàn chū	to stand out (veins, etc.)
爭辯	zhēngbiàn	to argue in one's own defence
竊	qiè	to steal (class.)
君子固窮	jūn zǐ gù qiúng	This is a quotation from the *Confucian Analects* 15/2 which runs. 君子固窮，小人窮斯濫矣 "It is to be expected that the gentleman should be in straitened circumstances. Petty men in straitened circumstances would stop at nothing."
哄笑	hōngxiào	uproar
快活	kuàihuó	good humour, merriment
背地裏	bèidìlǐ	behind his back
進學	jìnxüé	to pass the lowest grade examination and to become a 生員 shēng yüán (commonly known as 秀才 xìu cái)

討飯了。幸而寫得一筆好字，便替人家鈔鈔書，換一
碗飯喫。可惜他又有一樣壞脾氣，便是好喝懶做。坐
不到幾天，便連人和書籍紙張筆硯，一齊失蹤。如是
幾次，叫他鈔書的人也沒有了。孔乙己沒有法，便免
不了偶然做些偷竊的事。但他在我們店裏，品行卻比
別人都好，就是從不拖欠；雖然間或沒有現錢，暫時
記在粉板上，但不出一月，定然清還，從粉板上拭去
了孔乙己的名字。

　　孔乙己喝過半碗酒，漲紅的臉色漸漸復了原，旁
人便又問道，『孔乙己，你當眞認識字麼？』孔乙己
看着問他的人，顯出不屑置辯的神氣。他們便接着說
道，『你怎的連半個秀才也撈不到呢？』孔乙己立刻
顯出頹唐不安模樣，臉上籠上了一層灰色，嘴裏說些
話；這回可是全是之乎者也之類，一些不懂了。在這
時候，眾人也都哄笑起來：店內外充滿了快活的空氣。

　　在這些時候，我可以附和着笑，掌櫃是決不責備
的。而且掌櫃見了孔乙己，也每每這樣問他，引人發
笑。孔乙己自己知道不能和他們談天，便只好向孩子
說話。有一回對我說道，『你讀過書麼？』我略略點
一點頭。他說，『讀過書，……我便考你一考。茴香
豆的茴字，怎樣寫的？』我想，討飯一樣的人，也配
考我麼？便回過臉去，不再理會。孔乙己等了許久，
很懇切的說道，『不能寫罷？……我教給你，記着！
這些字應該記着。將來做掌櫃的時候，寫賬要用。』
我暗想我和掌櫃的等級還很遠呢，而且我們掌櫃也從

不會營生	bú huì yíngshēng	no good at managing one's affairs, unable to make a living
幸而	xìng' ér	fortunate for him
寫得一筆好字	xiě de yì bǐ haǒ zì	to write a good hand
壞脾氣	huài píqì	bad habit
好喝懶做	hào hē lǎn zuò	bone lazy (though he would not mind drinking)
連 a 和 b	lián a hé b	a, b and all
書籍	shūjí	books
紙張	zhǐzhāng	(sheets of) paper
硯	yàn	inkstone
失踪	shīzōng	to disappear without trace
免不了	miǎn bù liǎo	it is only to be expected
品行	pǐnxìng	conduct
拖欠	tuōqiàn	to be in arrears
間或	jiànhuò	very occasionally
現錢	xiànqián	ready cash
粉板	fěnbǎn	blackboard
不出……	bù chū . . .	within . . .
還清	huán qīng	to clear a debt
復原	fù yüán	to return to normal
當眞	dāngzhēn	really (expressive of incredulity)
置辯	zhì biàn	to put forth arguments in one's own defence
撈	lāo	to manage to scrounge, to gain
頽唐	tuítáng	dejected
籠上	lóng shàng	to be covered with, to be encased with (colour, smoke)
附和	fùhè	to chime in, to echo
責備	zébèi	to tell off, to take to task
每每	měiměi	very often (cf. 每 which is more literary)
引	yǐn	to provoke, to spark off, to lead to
談天	tántiān	to chat
只好	zhǐhǎo	to have to be content with
我想	wǒ xiǎng	I thought to myself
討飯	tǎofàn	beggar
配	pèi	to be in a position to, to be fit to
也配考我嗎	yě pèi kǎo wǒ mā ?	what a cheek for (a chap no better than a beggar) to test me
回過臉去	huí guò liǎn qǜ	to turn one's face away (in displeasure)
不再理會	bú zài lǐhuì	to pay no further attention to
懇切	kěnqiè	earnest
賬	zhàng	accounts
等級	děngjí	grade

不將茴香豆上賬；又好笑，又不耐煩，懶懶的答他道，
『誰要你教，不是草頭底下一個來回的回字麼？』孔
乙己顯出極高興的樣子，將兩個指頭的長指甲敲着櫃
臺，點頭說，『對呀對呀！……回字有四樣寫法，你
知道麼？』我愈不耐煩了，努着嘴走遠。孔乙己剛用
指甲蘸了酒，想在櫃上寫字，見我毫不熱心，便又歎
一口氣，顯出極惋惜的樣子。

　　有幾回，鄰舍孩子聽得笑聲，也趕熱鬧，圍住了
孔乙己。他便給他們茴香豆喫，一人一顆。孩子喫完
豆，仍然不散，眼睛都望着碟子。孔乙己着了慌，伸
開五指將碟子罩住，彎腰下去說道，『不多了，我已
經不多了。』直起身又看一看豆，自己搖頭說，『不
多不多！多乎哉？不多也。』于是這一羣孩子都在笑
聲裏走散了。

　　孔乙己是這樣的使人快活，可是沒有他，別人也
便這麼過。

　　有一天，大約是中秋前的兩三天，掌櫃正在慢慢
的結賬，取下粉板，忽然說，『孔乙己長久沒有來了。
還欠十九個錢呢！』我纔也覺得他的確長久沒有來了。
一個喝酒的人說道，『他怎麼會來？……他打折了腿
了。』掌櫃說，『哦！』『他總仍舊是偷。這一回，
是自己發昏，竟偷到丁舉人家裏去了。他家的東西，
偷得的麼？』『後來怎麼樣？』『怎麼樣？先寫服辯，
後來是打，打了大半夜，再打折了腿。』『後來呢？』
『後來打折了腿了。』『打折了怎樣呢？』『怎樣？
……誰曉得？許是死了。』掌櫃也不再問，仍然慢慢

好笑	hǎoxiào	(to find it) ridiculous, amused
不耐煩	bú nàifán	to have no time for something, to be fed up with
草頭	cǎo tóu	with the "++" radical on top
指甲	zhǐ jiǎ	(finger) nails
敲	qiāo	to tap, to knock
點頭	diǎn tóu	to nod one's head
努着嘴	nǔ zhe zǔi	with pouted lips
蘸	zhàn	to dip (in a liquid)
熱心	rèxīn	enthusiastic, enthusiasm
惋惜	wǎnxī	to find it a great pity
趕熱鬧	gǎn rènào	to rush to join in the fun
着了慌	zhāo le huāng	to get into a panic
罩	zhào	a bell-shaped cover – to cover up with such a cover (cf. 籠)
彎腰	wān yāo	to bend down
直起身	zhí qǐ shēn	to straighten up one's body
便這麼過	biàn zhème guò	to make do (without)
中秋	zhōngqiū	mid-autumn festival (15th day of 8th moon)
正在	zhèngzài	in the process of doing something
結賬	jié zhàng	to make up the accounts
發昏	fā hūn	to be out of his senses
偷到……	tōu dào . . .	(of all places) to get round to stealing from . . .
偷得的嗎？	tōu dé de ma ?	He was asking for trouble stealing from . . .
服辯	fúbiàn	confession
半夜	bàn yè	half the night (大 bigger – more than)

的算他的賬。

　　中秋過後，秋風是一天涼比一天，看看將近初冬；我整天的靠着火，也須穿上棉襖了。一天的下半天，沒有一個顧客，我正合了眼坐着。忽然間聽得一個聲音，『溫一碗酒。』這聲音雖然極低，卻很耳熟。看時又全沒有人。站起來向外一望，那孔乙己便在櫃臺下對了門檻坐着。他臉上黑而且瘦，已經不成樣子；穿一件破夾襖，盤着兩腿，下面墊一個蒲包，用草繩在肩上掛住；見了我，又說道，『溫一碗酒。』掌櫃也伸出頭去，一面說，『孔乙己麼？你還欠十九個錢呢！』孔乙己很頹唐的仰面答道，『這……下回還清罷。這一回是現錢，酒要好。』掌櫃仍然同平常一樣，笑着對他說，『孔乙己，你又偷了東西了！』但他這回卻不十分分辯，單說了一句『不要取笑！』『取笑？要是不偷，怎麼會打斷腿？』孔乙己低聲說道，『跌斷，跌，跌……』他的眼色，很像懇求掌櫃，不要再提。此時已經聚集了幾個人，便和掌櫃都笑了。我溫了酒，端出去，放在門檻上。他從破衣袋裏摸出四文大錢，放在我手裏，見他滿手是泥，原來他便用這手走來的。不一會，他喝完酒，便又在旁人的說笑聲中，坐着用這手慢慢走去了。

　　自此以後，又長久沒有看見孔乙己。到了年關，掌櫃取下粉板說，『孔乙己還欠十九個錢呢！』到第二年的端午，又說『孔乙己還欠十九個錢呢！』到中秋可是沒有說，再到年關也沒有看見他。

　　我到現在終于沒有見——大約孔乙己的確死了。

一天涼比一天＝一天比一天涼

看看	kàn kàn	soon
初冬	chūdōng	early winter
整天	zhēngtiān	the whole day
靠火	kào huǒ	to be by the fire
棉襖	mián ǎo	padded jacket
合了眼	hé le yǎn	with eyes closed
耳熟	ěrshú	familiar to the ear, to sound familiar
門檻	ménkǎn	door sill
不成樣子	bù chéng yàngzi	beyond description, like nothing on earth
盤着腿	pán zhe tuǐ	cross-legged
墊	diàn	to cushion (underneath)
蒲包	púbāo	a rush sack
伸出頭	shēn chū tóu	to pop one's head out
酒要好	jiǔ yào hǎo	it has to be good wine
取笑	qǔxiào	to make fun of
跌	diē	to fall
眼色	yǎnsè	the expression in his eyes
懇求	kěnqiú	to beseech
端	duān	to carry carefully with both hands (to avoid spilling)
摸	mō	to grope for
滿	mǎn	(pref.) all over
原來	yüánlái	I did not realise until then that he actually
不一會	bù yì huǐr	in a moment
年關	niánguān	the end of the year; (guan suggests an obstacle difficult to get through because traditionally one is supposed to pay off all one's debts by the end of the year)
端午	duānwǔ	Dragon Boat Festival (5th day of the 5th moon)

藥

一

　　秋天的後半夜，月亮下去了，太陽還沒有出，只剩下一片烏藍的天；除了夜遊的東西，什麼都睡着。華老栓忽然坐起身。擦着火柴，點上遍身油膩的燈盞，茶館的兩間屋子裏，便瀰滿了靑白的光。

　　『小栓的爹，你就去麼?』是一個老女人的聲音。裏邊的小屋子裏，也發出一陣咳嗽。

　　『唔。』老栓一面聽，一面應，一面扣上衣服；伸手過去說，『你給我罷。』

　　華大媽在枕頭底下掏了半天，掏出一包洋錢，交給老栓，老栓接了，抖抖的裝入衣袋，又在外面按了兩下；便點上燈籠，吹熄燈盞，走向裏屋子去了。那屋子裏面，正在窸窸窣窣的響，接着便是一通咳嗽。老栓候他平靜下去，纔低低的叫道，『小栓……你不要起來。……店麼？你娘會安排的。』

　　老栓聽得兒子不再說話，料他安心睡了；便出了門，走到街上。街上黑沉沉的一無所有，只有一條灰白的路，看得分明。燈光照着他的兩脚，一前一後的走。有時也遇到幾隻狗，可是一隻也沒有叫。天氣比屋子裏冷得多了；老栓倒覺爽快，彷彿一旦變了少年，得了神通，有給人生命的本領似的，跨步格外高遠。

藥　Yào

後半夜	hòu bàn yè	the latter half of the night
一片	yí piàn	an expanse
烏藍	wūlán	darkish blue
夜遊的東西	yè yóu de dōngxi	creatures that roam by night
擦着火柴	cā jě huǒchái	to have struck a match
遍身	biàn shēn	all over the body
油膩	yóunì	greasy
燈盞	dēngzhǎn	oil-lamp
瀰滿（漫）	mí mǎn (màn)	to be filled with (fog, smoke, light)
你就去嗎？		Are you going this minute?
一陣	yí zhèn	a fit, a spell
掏	táo	to fumble (in pocket)
抖抖的	dǒu dǒu de	trembling
裝入	zhuāng rù	to stuff into
按	àn	to press (here "to pat")
吹熄	chuī xī	to blow out
窸窸窣窣	xī xī sū sū	rustling (here of bedclothes)
一通	yì tōng	a bout, round (often a measure word for letters in literary usage)
平靜下去	píngjìng xià qù	to subside, to calm down
店嗎？		as for the shop — if it is the shop you are worrying about
安排	ānpái	to see to it, to arrange satisfactorily
料	liào	to reckon, to think, to conjecture
安心	ānxīn	with one's mind at ease
黑沉沉	hēichénchén	darkness (chen chen suggests heaviness)
一無所有	yì wú suǒ yǒu	an absolute void
看得分明	kàn de fēnmíng	could be clearly made out
爽快	shuǎngkuài	refreshing
一旦	yí dàn	all of a sudden
神通	shéntōng	magical powers
本領	běnlǐng	special ability
跨步	kuà bù	to step out
格外	géwài	exceptionally, more than usual

而且路也愈走愈分明，天也愈走愈亮了。

　　老栓正在專心走路，忽然喫了一驚，遠遠裏看見一條丁字街，明明白白橫着。他便退了幾步，尋到一家關着門的鋪子，蹩進簷下，靠門立住了。好一會，身上覺得有些發冷。

　　『哼，老頭子。』

　　『倒高興……。』

　　老栓又喫一驚，睜眼看時，幾個人從他面前過去了。一個還回頭看他，樣子不甚分明，但很像久餓的人見了食物一般，眼裏閃出一種攫取的光。老栓看看燈籠，已經熄了。按一按衣袋，硬硬的還在。仰起頭兩面一望，只見許多古怪的人，三三兩兩，鬼似的在那里徘徊；定睛再看，卻也看不出什麼別的奇怪。

　　沒有多久，又見幾個兵，在那邊走動；衣服前後的一個大白圓圈，遠地裏也看得清楚，走過面前的，並且看出號衣上暗紅色的鑲邊。——一陣脚步聲響，一眨眼，已經擁過了一大簇人。那三三兩兩的人，也忽然合作一堆，潮一般向前趕；將到丁字街口，便突然立住，簇成一個半圓。

　　老栓也向那邊看，卻只見一堆人的後背；頸項都伸得很長，彷彿許多鴨，被無形的手捏住了的，向上提着。靜了一會，似乎有點聲音，便又動搖起來，轟的一聲，都向後退；一直散到老栓立着的地方，幾乎將他擠倒了。

　　『喂！一手交錢，一手交貨！』一個渾身黑色的

專心	zhuānxīn	single-minded
丁字街	dīngzì jiē	T-junction
蹩	bié	to slink
好一會		a good while
發冷	fālěng	shivering
久餓	jiǔ è	starved for long
攫取	jüé qǔ	predatory
硬硬的	yìng yìng de	that hard thing (i.e., the silver money)
古怪	gǔguài	odd, strange
徘徊	páihuái	to pace up and down
定睛再看	dìng jīng zài kàn	to steady one's gaze and give another look
鑲邊	xiāngbiān	border
一眨眼	yì zhǎ yǎn	in the twinkling of an eye
擁過	yǒng guò	(of crowd) to come rushing across
簇	cù	a conglomeration, a crowd
一堆	yì duī	a heap
合作一堆		to come together in a heap
頸項	jǐng xiàng	neck (pl here)
捏	niè	to grab hold of, grasp
轟	hōng	descriptive of thunderous or rumbling noise
一手交錢一手交貨	yì shǒu jiāo qián yì shǒu jiāo huò	You hand over the money and I'll hand over the goods at the same time
渾身	húnshēn	all over (often describing the uniform colour of one's clothes), from top to bottom

人，站在老栓面前，眼光正像兩把刀，刺得老栓縮小了一半。那人一隻大手，向他攤着；一隻手卻撮着一個鮮紅的饅頭，那紅的還是一點一點的往下滴。

老栓慌忙摸出洋錢，抖抖的想交給他，卻又不敢去接他的東西。那人便焦急起來，嚷道，『怕什麼？怎的不拿！』老栓還躊躇着；黑的人便搶過燈籠，一把扯下紙罩，裹了饅頭，塞與老栓；一手抓過洋錢，捏一捏，轉身去了。嘴裏哼着說，『這老東西……。』

『這給誰治病的呀?』老栓也似乎聽得有人問他，但他並不答應；他的精神，現在只在一個包上，彷彿抱着一個十世單傳的嬰兒，別的事情，都已置之度外了。他現在要將這包裹的新的生命，移植到他家裏，收穫許多幸福。太陽也出來了；在他面前，顯出一條大道，直到他家中，後面也照見丁字街頭破匾上『古□亭口』這四個黯淡的金字。

二

老栓走到家，店面早經收拾乾淨，一排一排的茶桌，滑溜溜的發光。但是沒有客人：只有小栓坐在裏排的桌前喫飯，大粒的汗，從額上滾下，夾襖也帖住了脊心，兩塊肩胛骨高高凸出，印成一個陽文的『八』字。老栓見這樣子，不免皺一皺展開的眉心。他的女

縮小	suō xiǎo	to shrink in size
攤着	tān je	outspread
撮	cuō	to hold between the fingers
鮮紅	xiān hóng	bright red, crimson
滴	dī	to drip; a drop
摸出	mō chū	to grope for and produce
焦急起來	jiāojí qǐ lái	to get impatient
嚷	rǎng	to yell
躊躇	chóuchú	to hesitate
搶過	qiǎng guò	to snatch (thing) over
一把	yì bǎ	with one grab
扯下	chě xià	to tear off, to rip off
紙罩	zhǐzhào	the paper (lamp) shade
塞	sāi	to thrust into, to thrust at
抓	zhuā	to grab hold of
捏一捏	niē yi niē	to give (it) a squeeze (to see if it was silver)
哼	hēng	to mutter
精神	jīngshén	mind
他的精神只在 十世單傳	shí shì dān chuán	his whole mind was centred on a single male heir for each generation over ten generations
置之度外	zhì zhì dù wài	to exclude from one's calculations, to cease to concern oneself with, to put out of one's mind
移植	yí zhí	to transplant
收穫	shōu huò	to reap
匾	biǎn	a plaque
古口亭口		The real name was 古軒亭 It was a kind of pavilion. □ represents a missing character. 口 means 'entrance to' or 'junction of'
黯淡	àndàn	faint, lacklustre
金字	jīn zì	gold characters
店面	diànmiàn	shop front
早經(早已)	zǎo jīng	long since
收拾	shōushí	to tidy up
乾淨	gānjìng	tidy, clean
滑溜溜	huáliuliu	so smooth that it is slippery to the touch
裏	lǐ	inner
裏排	lǐ pái	the back row
粒	lì	bead; grain
滾下	gǔn xià	to roll off
帖(貼)住	tiē zhù	sticking to
脊心	jǐxīn	spine
肩胛骨	jiānjiǎ gǔ	shoulder blade
凸出	tū chū	to protrude, to jut out
陽文	yáng wén	embossed, carved in relief
皺眉	zhòu méi	to frown
展開	zhǎn kāi	to spread out
眉心	méixīn	space between the eyebrows

人，從竈下急急走出，睜着眼睛，嘴唇有些發抖。

『得了麼？』

『得了。』

兩個人一齊走進竈下，商量了一會，華大媽便出去了，不多時，拏着一片老荷葉回來，攤在桌上。老栓也打開燈籠罩，用荷葉重新包了那紅的饅頭。小栓也喫完飯，他的母親慌忙說：——

『小栓——你坐着，不要到這里來。』

一面整頓了竈火，老栓便把一個碧綠的包，一個紅紅白白的破燈籠，一同塞在竈裏；一陣紅黑的火燄過去時，店屋裏散滿了一種奇怪的香味。

『好香！你們喫什麼點心呀？』這是駝背五少爺到了。這人每天總在茶館裏過日，來得最早，去得最遲，此時恰恰蹩到臨街的壁角的桌邊，便坐下問話，然而沒有人答應他。『炒米粥麼？』仍然沒有人應。老栓匆匆走出，給他泡上茶。

『小栓進來罷！』華大媽叫小栓進了裏面的屋子，中間放好一條凳，小栓坐了。他的母親端過一碟烏黑的圓東西，輕輕說：——

『喫下去罷，——病便好了。』

小栓撮起這黑東西，看了一會，似乎拏着自己的性命一般，心裏說不出的奇怪。十分小心的拗開了，焦皮裏面竄出一道白氣，白氣散了，是兩半個白麪的饅頭。——不多工夫，已經全在肚裏了，卻全忘了什麼味；面前只剩下一張空盤。他的旁邊，一面立着他

女人	nǚrén	wife
竈下	zào xià	in front of the cooking range
重新	chóngxīn	afresh (chong, pref. re-)
慌忙	huāngmáng	hastily in confusion
整頓	zhěngdùn	to put in order
碧綠	bì lǜ	jade green
駝背	tuóbèi	hunchbacked
恰恰	qiàqià	just (at the moment)
炒	chǎo	to roast something in a pan while constantly turning it over
粥	zhōu	rice cooked with a lot of water to form a porridge
匆匆	cōng cōng	hurriedly
泡茶	pào chá	to infuse tea
凳	dèng	stool, (backless) bench
拗開	aò kāi	to break by bending (dialectal)
焦	jiāo	burned, scorched
竄出	cuàn chū	to dart out, to flee (like a mouse)
工夫	gōngfu	time

的父親，一面立着他的母親，兩人的眼光，都彷彿要在他身裏注進什麼又要取出什麼似的；便禁不住心跳起來，按着胸膛，又是一陣咳嗽。

『睡一會罷，——便好了。』

小栓依他母親的話，咳着睡了。華大媽候他喘氣平靜，纔輕輕的給他蓋上了滿幅補釘的夾被。

三

店裏坐着許多人，老栓也忙了，提着大銅壺，一趟一趟的給客人沖茶；兩個眼眶，都圍着一圈黑線。

『老栓，你有些不舒服麼？——你生病麼？』一個花白鬍子的人說。

『沒有。』

『沒有？——我想笑嘻嘻的，原也不像……』花白鬍子便取消了自己的話。

『老栓只是忙。要是他的兒子……』駝背五少爺話還未完，突然闖進了一個滿臉橫肉的人，披一件玄色布衫，散着紐釦，用很寬的玄色腰帶，胡亂綑在腰間。剛進門，便對老栓嚷道：——

『喫了麼？好了麼？老栓，就是運氣了你！你運氣，要不是我信息靈……。』

老栓一手提了茶壺，一手恭恭敬敬的垂着；笑嘻嘻的聽。滿座的人，也都恭恭敬敬的聽。華大媽也黑着眼眶，笑嘻嘻的送出茶碗茶葉來，加上一個橄欖，老栓便去沖了水。

『這是包好！這是與衆不同的。你想，趁熱的拏

眼光	yǎnguāng	gaze
注進	zhù jìn	to inject, to infuse
禁不住	jìn bú zhù	unable to control oneself from (doing)
咳嗽	késòu	cough
喘氣	chuǎn qì	panting, rough breathing
滿幅補釘	mǎn fú bǔdīng	patched all over
銅壺	tóng hú	copper kettle
一趟	yí tàng	once, one time (e.g. counting number of trips)
沖茶	chōng chá	to add water to the tea
眼眶	yǎnkuàng	socket of the eye
圈	quān	circle
笑嘻嘻	xiàoxìxi	grinning all over
取消	qǔxiāo	to cancel
突然	tūrán	suddenly, without warning
闖進	chuǎng jìn	to burst in
滿臉橫肉	mǎn liǎn héng ròu	with flesh bulging all over the face (descriptive of a bully)
披	pī	to wear, to drape over the shoulder
玄色	xüán sè	black
散着	sǎn je	loose
紐扣	nǐukòu	button
綑	kǔn	to bind
運氣	yùnqì	good luck (here used, rather unusually, as a verb)
信息靈通	xìnxi língtōng	to be in the know
恭恭敬敬	gōnggōng jìngjìng	very respectfully
滿座的人	mǎn zuò de rén	everyone present
橄欖	gǎnlǎn	olive
包	bāo	(pref.) guaranteed to
與衆不同	yǔ zhòng bù tóng	quite different from the run of the mill
趁＋a＋b	chèn	(pref.) to do b while it is still a

來，趁熱喫下。』橫肉的人只是嚷。

　　『眞的呢，要沒有康大叔照顧，怎麼會這樣……』
華大媽也很感激的謝他。

　　『包好，包好！這樣的趁熱喫下。這樣的人血饅
頭，什麼癆病都包好！』

　　華大媽聽到『癆病』這兩個字，變了一點臉色，
似乎有些不高興；但又立刻堆上笑，搭赸着走開了。
這康大叔卻沒有覺察，仍然提高了喉嚨只是嚷，嚷得
裏面睡着的小栓也合夥咳嗽起來。

　　『原來你家小栓碰到了這樣的好運氣了。這病自
然一定全好；怪不得老栓整天的笑着呢。』花白鬍子
一面說，一面走到康大叔面前，低聲下氣的問道，
『康大叔——聽說今天結果的一個犯人，便是夏家的
孩子，那是誰的孩子？究竟是什麼事？』

　　『誰的?不就是夏四奶奶的兒子麼?那個小傢伙!』
康大叔見眾人都聳起耳朵聽他，便格外高興，橫肉塊
塊飽綻，越發大聲說，『這小東西不要命，不要就是
了。我可是這一回一點沒有得到好處；連剝下來的衣
服，都給管牢的紅眼睛阿義拏去了。——第一要算我
們栓叔運氣;第二是夏三爺賞了二十五兩雪白的銀子，
獨自落腰包，一文不花。』

　　小栓慢慢的從小屋子走出，兩手按了胸口，不住
的咳嗽；走到竈下，盛出一碗冷飯，泡上熱水，坐下
便喫。華大媽跟着他走，輕輕的問道，『小栓你好些
麼？——你仍舊只是肚餓？……』

趁熱喫下		to get it inside you while it is hot
只是		to do nothing but
照顧	zhàogù	kind help
感激	gǎnji	grateful
癆病	láo bìng	consumption
變臉色	biàn liǎnsè	to turn pale
堆上笑	duī shàng xiào	to pile on a smile
搭赸	dāshàn	in an embarrassed situation, to say something to cover up one's embarrassment (cf. 訕訕)
覺察	jüéchá	to notice, to discover
提高了喉嚨	tí gāo le hóulóng	to raise one's voice
合夥	héhuǒ	to go into partnership – to join in
碰到	pèng dào	to meet with
結果	jiéguǒ	end, to put an end to, to finish off, hence to kill
究竟	jiūjìng	in the final analysis, really
不就是……麼		who (or what) else except . . .
小傢伙	xiǎo jiāhuǒ	young rascal
聳起耳朵	sǒng qǐ ěrduō	to cock one's ears
飽綻	bǎozhàn	to bulge out
越發	yüèfā	the more so
不要命	bú yào mìng	to think nothing of throwing away one's life
好處	hǎochù	what is to one's advantage
剝	bāo	to strip, to peel off
牢	láo	gaol
賞	shǎng	to give a reward or gratuity
落腰包	lào yāobāo	to pocket
花	huā	to spend
盛	chéng	to put into, to fill container; (container) holds
冷飯	lěngfàn	cold (left-over) rice
輕輕的	cīngcīng de	lightly, softly

　　『包好，包好！』康大叔瞥了小栓一眼，仍然回過臉，對衆人說，『夏三爺眞是乖角兒，要是他不先告官，連他滿門抄斬。現在怎樣？銀子！——這小東西也眞不成東西！關在牢裏，還要勸牢頭造反。』

　　『阿呀，那還了得。』坐在後排的一個二十多歲的人，很現出氣憤模樣。

　　『你要曉得紅眼睛阿義是去盤盤底細的，他卻和他攀談了。他說：這大淸的天下是我們大家的。你想：這是人話麼？紅眼睛原知道他家裏只有一個老娘，可是沒有料到他竟會那麼窮，搾不出一點油水，已經氣破肚皮了。他還要老虎頭上搔癢，便給他兩個嘴巴！』

　　『義哥是一手好拳棒，這兩下，一定夠他受用了。』壁角的駝背忽然高興起來。

　　『他這賤骨頭打不怕，還要說可憐可憐哩。』

　　花白鬍子的人說，『打了這種東西，有什麼可憐呢？』

　　康大叔顯出看他不上的樣子，冷笑着說，『你沒有聽淸我的話；看他神氣，是說阿義可憐哩！』

　　聽着的人的眼光，忽然有些板滯；話也停頓了。小栓已經喫完飯，喫得滿身流汗，頭上都冒出蒸氣來。

　　『阿義可憐——瘋話，簡直是發了瘋了。』花白鬍子恍然大悟似的說。

　　『發了瘋了。』二十多歲的人也恍然大悟的說。

　　店裏的坐客，便又現出活氣，談笑起來。小栓也趁着熱鬧，拚命咳嗽；康大叔走上前，拍他肩膀說：——

瞥一眼	piē yì yǎn	to cast a sidelong glance
乖角兒	guāi jiǎor	a smart one
告官	gàoguān	to bring an accusation (here, to inform against)
滿門抄斬	mǎn mén chāo zhǎn	all members of a family put to death and all their property confiscated
眞不成東西		a real bad one
牢頭	láotóu	gaoler
造反	zàofǎn	rebellion (against the emperor)
那還了得	nà hái liǎo dé	whatever next
氣憤	qìfèn	angry, indignant
盤盤底細	pán pán dǐxì	to find out all about (someone)
攀談	pāntán	to strike up a conversation
天下	tiānxià	Empire
人話	rén huà	words of a human being
搾出油水	zhà chū yóushuǐ	squeeze something out of
氣破肚皮	qì pò dùpí	so angry that his belly nearly exploded
老虎頭上搔癢	lǎohǔ tóu shàng sāo yǎng	asking for it
嘴巴	zuǐbā	a smack on the mouth
一手好拳棒	yì shǒu hǎo quánbàng	good at armed and unarmed combat
壁角	bì jiǎo	in the corner by the wall
賤骨頭	jiàn gǔtóu	bones born to be beaten
可憐	kělián	pitiable, (of a person) one feels sorry for
看不上	kàn bú shàng	to look down upon
聽清	tīng qīng	to hear clearly
板滯	bǎnzhì	wooden, glazed (look)
停頓	tíngdùn	to come to a standstill
冒出	mào chū	to rise up out of
瘋話	fēng huà	crazy talk
恍然大悟	huǎngrán dà wù	to see the light suddenly

『包好！小栓——你不要這麼咳。包好！』

『瘋了。』駝背五少爺點着頭說。

四

西關外靠着城根的地面，本是一塊官地；中間歪歪斜斜一條細路，是貪走便道的人，用鞋底造成的，但卻成了自然的界限。路的左邊，都埋着死刑和瘐斃的人，右邊是窮人的叢塚。兩面都已埋到層層疊疊，宛然闊人家裏祝壽時候的饅頭。

這一年的清明，分外寒冷；楊柳纔吐出半粒米大的新芽。天明未久，華大媽已在右邊的一坐新墳前面，排出四碟菜，一碗飯，哭了一場。化過紙，呆呆的坐在地上；彷彿等候什麼似的，但自己也說不出等候什麼。微風起來，吹動他短髮，確乎比去年白得多了。

小路上又來了一個女人，也是半白頭髮，襤褸的衣裙；提一個破舊的朱漆圓籃，外掛一串紙錠，三步一歇的走。忽然見華大媽坐在地上看他，便有些躊躇，慘白的臉上，現出些羞愧的顏色；但終于硬着頭皮，走到左邊的一坐墳前，放下了籃子。

那墳與小栓的墳，一字兒排着，中間只隔一條小路。華大媽看他排好四碟菜，一碗飯，立着哭了一通，化過紙錠；心裏暗暗地想，『這墳裏的也是兒子了。』那老女人徘徊觀望了一回，忽然手腳有些發抖，蹌蹌跟跟退下幾步，瞪着眼只是發怔。

華大媽見這樣子，生怕他傷心到快要發狂了；便忍不住立起身，跨過小路，低聲對他說，『你這位老

西關	xī guān	the west gate
城根	chénggēn	close by the city wall
歪歪斜斜	wāi wāi xié xié	crooked
便道	biàndào	short cut
界限	jièxiàn	boundary
死刑	sǐ xíng	capital punishment
瘐斃	yǔ bì	to waste away and die in prison (lit.)
叢塚	cóng zhǒng	cluster of graves, mass grave
層層疊疊	céng céng dié dié	tier upon tier
闊	kuò	well to do
祝壽	zhù shòu	to celebrate birthday
清明	qīngmíng	festival for visiting graves of deceased ancestors (April 5th or 6th)
分外	fènwài	unusually (cf. gé wài)
楊柳	yánglǐu	willow
芽	yá	bud
化	huà	(in this context) to burn; to transform, to disintegrate
紙	zhǐ	(in this context) paper money, (cf. zhǐ ding)
呆呆	dāi dāi	vacantly
確乎	qüèhū	without doubt
襤褸	lánlǔ	tattered
朱漆	zhū qī	vermilion-coloured lacquer
紙綻	zhǐding	paper money
三步一歇	sān bù yī xiē	resting frequently
慘白	cǎnbái	pale, drained of all blood
羞愧	xiūkuì	shame
硬着頭皮	yìng je tóupí	to brace oneself (for something unpleasant)
觀望	guānwàng	to look on, to look up and down (not taking any action)
發抖	fā dǒu	to tremble
蹌蹌跟跟	qiàng qiàng làng làng	tottering
瞪着眼	dèng je yǎn	with staring eyes
發怔	fā zhēng	lost, dumbfounded
發狂	fā kuáng	to go mad
跨過	kuà guò	to step over

奶奶不要傷心了，——我們還是回去罷。』

那人點一點頭，眼睛仍然向上瞪着；也低聲吃吃的說道，『你看，——看這是什麼呢？』

華大媽跟了他指頭看去，眼光便到了前面的墳，這墳上草根還沒有全合，露出一塊一塊的黃土，煞是難看。再往上仔細看時，卻不覺也喫一驚；——分明有一圈紅白的花，圍着那尖圓的墳頂。

他們的眼睛都已老花多年了，但望這紅白的花，卻還能明白看見。花也不很多，圓圓的排成一個圈，不很精神，倒也整齊。華大媽忙看他兒子和別人的墳，卻只有不怕冷的幾點青白小花，零星開着；便覺得心裏忽然感到一種不足和空虛，不願意根究。那老女人又走近幾步，細看了一遍，自言自語的說，『這沒有根，不像自己開的。——這地方有誰來呢？孩子不會來玩；——親戚本家早不來了。——這是怎麼一回事呢？』他想了又想，忽然流下淚來，大聲說道：——

『瑜兒，他們都寃枉了你，你還是忘不了，傷心不過，今天特意顯點靈，要我知道麼？』他四面一看，只見一隻烏鴉，站在一株沒有葉的樹上，便接着說，『我知道了。——瑜兒，可憐他們坑了你，他們將來總有報應，天都知道；你閉了眼睛就是了。——你如果眞在這里，聽到我的話，——便教這烏鴉飛上你的墳頂，給我看罷。』

微風早經停息了；枯草支支直立，有如銅絲。一絲發抖的聲音，在空氣中愈顫愈細，細到沒有，周圍

煞是	shāshì	really
難看	nánkàn	ugly, unsightly
仔細	zìxì	carefully
老花	lǎohuā	long sightedness due to age
精神	jingshén	vigorous
整齊	zhěngqí	neat and tidy
零星	língxing	dotted here and there
不足	bùzú	dissatisfaction
空虛	kōngxū	emptiness
根究	gēnjiu	to get to the bottom of (something)
親戚	qīnqi	relations
本家	běnjiā	clansmen descended from a common ancestor
冤枉	yüānwǎng	to wrong
不過	búguò	(suff.) utmost
顯靈	xiǎn líng	(spirit) manifesting itself
坑	kēng	to dig a pit and bury alive (here used metaphorically)
報應	bàoyìng	desert, due punishment or (more rarely) reward
銅絲	tóng sī	copper wire
一絲	yì sī	a thread (here, of sound)

便都是死一般靜。兩人站在枯草叢裏，仰面看那烏鴉；那烏鴉也在筆直的樹枝間，縮着頭，鐵鑄一般站着。

許多的工夫過去了；上墳的人漸漸增多，幾個老的小的，在土墳間出沒。

華大媽不知怎的，似乎卸下了一挑重擔，便想到要走；一面勸着說：『我們還是回去罷。』

那老女人歎一口氣，無精打采的收起飯菜；又遲疑了一刻，終于慢慢地走了。嘴裏自言自語的說，『這是怎麼一回事呢？……』

他們走不上二三十步遠，忽聽得背後『啞——』的一聲大叫；兩個人都竦然的回過頭，只見那烏鴉張開兩翅，一挫身，直向着遠處的天空，箭也似的飛去了。

筆直	bǐzhí	straight as a rod
縮	suō	to pull in, to shrink
鐵鑄	tiězhù	cast in iron
出沒	chūmò	to go in and out, now to be seen, now out of sight
卸	xiè	to put down, to be relieved of
重擔	zhòng dàn	heavy load
歎一口氣	tàn yì kǒu qì	to heave a sigh
無精打采	wú jīng dǎ cǎi	listlessly, dejected
遲疑	chíyí	to hesitate
竦然	sǒngrán	with hair standing on end, feeling eerie
翅	chì	wing
一挫身	yí cuò shēn	to lower itself ready for the upward spring

『沒有聲音，——小東西怎了？』

紅鼻子老拱手裏擎了一碗黃酒，說着，向間壁努一努嘴。藍皮阿五便放下酒碗，在他脊梁上用死勁的打了一掌，含含糊糊嚷道：——

『你……你你又在想心思……。』

原來魯鎮是僻靜地方，還有些古風：不上一更，大家便都關門睡覺。深更半夜沒有睡的只有兩家：一家是咸亨酒店，幾個酒肉朋友圍着櫃臺，喫喝得正高興；一家便是間壁的單四嫂子，他自從前年守了寡，便須專靠着自己的一雙手紡出棉紗來，養活他自己和他三歲的兒子，所以睡的也遲。

這幾天，確鑿沒有紡紗的聲音了。但夜深沒有睡的既然只有兩家，這單四嫂子家有聲音，便自然只有老拱們聽到，沒有聲音，也只有老拱們聽到。

老拱挨了打，彷彿很舒服似的喝了一大口酒，嗚嗚的唱起小曲來。

這時候，單四嫂子正抱着他的寶兒，坐在牀沿上，紡車靜靜的立在地上。黑沈沈的燈光，照着寶兒的臉，緋紅裏帶一點靑。單四嫂子心裏計算：神籤也求過了，願心也許過了，單方也喫過了，要是還不見效，怎麼好？——那只有去診何小仙了。但寶兒也許是日輕夜

擎	qíng	to hold up in one's hand
間壁（隔壁）	jiànbì (gé bì)	next door
脊梁	jíliang	spine
用死勁	yòng sǐ jìng	(of force) hard (by hitting without recoil)
含含糊糊	hán hán hú hú	indistinctly
想心思	xiǎng xīnsī	to turn one's thoughts to (dialectal)
僻靜	bèijìng	(of place) out of the way, remote, quiet, lonely
古風	gǔfēng	something of the simplicity in style of the ancients, old-fashioned
一更	yì gēng (jìng)	first watch (betwen 7 and 9 in the evening)
深更半夜	shēn gēng bàn yè	very late at night
酒肉朋友	jiǔ ròu péng yǒu	boon companion
守寡	shǒu guǎ	to become a widow; to live as a widow
靠	kào	to rely upon
紡	fǎng	to spin
棉紗	mián shā	cotton yarn
確鑿	qüèzuó	beyond any doubt whatsoever
嗚嗚	wū wū	sound of singing
牀沿	chuángyán	edge of the bed
緋紅	fēihóng	deep red, flushed
神籤	shén qiān	lots drawn (on which answer is given) when question is put to the gods
願心	yüànxīn	vow made to the gods
許	xǔ	to make (promise, vow)
單方	dānfāng	special remedy, effective prescription
診	zhěn	to look at a patient, to get a doctor to look at a patient

重，到了明天，太陽一出，熱也會退，氣喘也會平的：
這實在是病人常有的事。

　　單四嫂子是一個粗笨女人，不明白這『但』字的
可怕：許多壞事固然幸虧有了他纔變好，許多好事卻
也因爲有了他都弄糟。夏天夜短，老拱們嗚嗚的唱完
了不多時，東方已經發白；不一會，窗縫裏透進了銀
白色的曙光。

　　單四嫂子等候天明，卻不像別人這樣容易，覺得
非常之慢，寶兒的一呼吸，幾乎長過一年。現在居然
明亮了；天的明亮，壓倒了燈光，——看見寶兒的鼻
翼，已經一放一收的扇動。

　　單四嫂子知道不妙，暗暗叫一聲『阿呀！』心裏
計算：怎麼好？只有去診何小仙這一條路了。他雖然
是粗笨女人，心裏卻有決斷，便站起身，從木櫃子裏
掏出每天節省下來的十三個小銀元和一百八十銅錢，
都裝在衣袋裏，鎖上門，抱着寶兒直向何家奔過去。

　　天氣還早，何家已經坐着四個病人了。他摸出四
角銀元，買了號籤，第五個便輪到寶兒。何小仙伸開
兩個指頭按脈，指甲足有四寸多長，單四嫂子暗地納
罕，心裏計算：寶兒該有活命了。但總免不了着急，
忍不住要問，便局局促促的說：——

　　『先生，——我家的寶兒什麼病呀？』

　　『他中焦塞着。』

　　『不妨事麼？他……』

　　『先去喫兩帖。』

氣喘	qì chuǎn	shortness of breath, rough breathing
常有的事	cháng yǒu de shǐ	a common occurrence
粗笨	cūbèn	uneducated and not bright (both components suggest clumsily), slow-witted
幸虧	xìngkuī	thanks to, a good thing that . . .
透進	tòu jìn	to come through (of light)
曙光	shùgūang	light of dawn
居然	jūrán	actually (contrary to negative expectation)
壓倒	yā dǎo	to get the upper hand over, to overwhelm
鼻翼	bíyì	nostrils
不妙	búmiào	it looks bad, ominous, it bodes ill.
決斷	jüéduàn	resolve
節省	jiéshěng	to save, to economise
號籤	hàoqiān	a numbered slip
按脈	àn mài	to feel the pulse
納罕	nàhǎn	to wonder
該有活命	gāi yǒu huómìng	destined to be saved
局促	jǖcù	constrained, uneasy
中焦	zhōng jiāo	term in Chinese medicine: part of body where the stomach is
不妨事	bù fáng shǐ	nothing to cause concern
帖	tiě	a dose

『他喘不過氣來，鼻翅子都扇着呢。』

『這是火尅金……』

何小仙說了半句話，便閉上眼睛；單四嫂子也不好意思再問。在何小仙對面坐着的一個三十多歲的人，此時已經開好一張藥方，指着紙角上的幾個字說道：——

『這第一味保嬰活命丸，須是賈家濟世老店纔有！』

單四嫂子接過藥方，一面走，一面想。他雖是粗笨女人，卻知道何家與濟世老店與自己的家，正是一個三角點；自然是買了藥回去便宜了。于是又徑向濟世老店奔過去。店夥也翹了長指甲慢慢的看方，慢慢的包藥。單四嫂子抱了寶兒等着；寶兒忽然擎起小手來，用力拔他散亂着的一絡頭髮，這是從來沒有的舉動，單四嫂子怕得發怔。

太陽早出了。單四嫂子抱了孩子，帶着藥包，越走覺得越重；孩子又不住的掙扎，路也覺得越長。沒奈何坐在路旁一家公館的門檻上，休息了一會，衣服漸漸的冰着肌膚，纔知道自己出了一身汗；寶兒卻彷彿睡着了。他再起來慢慢地走，仍然支撐不得，耳朵邊忽然聽得人說：——

『單四嫂子，我替你抱勃囉！』似乎是藍皮阿五的聲音。

他擡頭看時，正是藍皮阿五，睡眼朦朧的跟着他走。

單四嫂子在這時候，雖然很希望降下一員天將，助他一臂之力，卻不願是阿五。但阿五有點俠氣，無

鼻翅子	bíchìzǐ	nostrils
尅	kè	to overcome
閉上	bì shàng	to close up
味	wèi	measure word for counting items on a prescription
保嬰活命丸	baǒ yǐng huó mǐng wán	name of a patent medicine: life-saver for babies
三角點	sān jiǎo diǎn	the points (dian) of a triangle (san jiao)
便宜	piányí	cheap – better buy – better plan
翹	qiáo	to curl upwards
一綹	yì liǔ	a tuft (of hair, beard)
舉動	jǔdòng	movement, action
掙扎	zhēngzhá	to struggle, to wriggle
沒奈何	méi nài hé	there is nothing for it but to . . .
公館	gōngguǎn	mansion, residence
支撐	zhīchēng	to manage to stay on one's feet
抱勃囉＝抱抱吧		(Shaoxing dialect)
睡眼矇矓	shuì yǎn ménglóng	half asleep
天將	tiān jiàng	celestial general
俠氣	xiáqì	something of a knight errant – helping the weak

論如何，總是偏要幫忙，所以推讓了一會，終于得了許可了。他便伸開臂膊，從單四嫂子的乳房和孩子中間，直伸下去，抱去了孩子。單四嫂子便覺乳房上發了一條熱，剎時間直熱到臉上和耳根。

　　他們兩人離開了二尺五寸多地，一同走着。阿五說些話，單四嫂子卻大半沒有答。走了不多時候，阿五又將孩子還給他，說是昨天與朋友約定的喫飯時候到了；單四嫂子便接了孩子。幸而不遠便是家，早看見對門的王九媽在街邊坐着，遠遠地說話：——

　　『單四嫂子，孩子怎了？——看過先生了麼？』

　　『看是看了。——王九媽，你有年紀，見的多，不如請你老法眼看一看，怎樣……』

　　『唔……』

　　『怎樣……？』

　　『唔……』王九媽端詳了一番，把頭點了兩點，搖了兩搖。

　　寶兒喫下藥，已經是午後了。單四嫂子留心看他神情，似乎彷彿平隱了不少；到得下午，忽然睜開眼叫一聲『媽！』又仍然合上眼，像是睡去了。他睡了一刻，額上鼻尖都沁出一粒一粒的汗珠，單四嫂子輕輕一摸，膠水般黏着手；慌忙去摸胸口，便禁不住嗚咽起來。

　　寶兒的呼吸從平穩變到沒有，單四嫂子的聲音也就從嗚咽變成號咷。這時聚集了幾堆人：門內是王九媽、藍皮阿五之類，門外是咸亨的掌櫃和紅鼻子老拱

偏要	piānyào	to insist on, to be contrary
推讓	tuīràng	to decline
臂膊	bèibó	arm
乳房	rǔfáng	breasts
刹時間	shà shí jiān	in a jiffy (刹 should be properly written 霎, as 刹 is pronounced cha)
法眼	fǎyǎn	experienced eye
端詳	duānxiáng	to size up
沁	qìn	to seep through
膠水	jiāoshuǐ	glue
黏	nián	to stick
平穩	píngwěn	steady
號咷	háotáo	to wail

之類。王九媽便發命令，燒了一串紙錢；又將兩條板
凳和五件衣服作抵，替單四嫂子借了兩塊洋錢，給幫
忙的人備飯。

　　第一個問題是棺木。單四嫂子還有一副銀耳環和
一支裹金的銀簪，都交給了咸亨的掌櫃，託他作一個
保，半現半賒的買一具棺木。藍皮阿五也伸出手來，
很願意自告奮勇；王九媽卻不許他，只准他明天擡棺
材的差使，阿五罵了一聲『老畜生』，快快的努了嘴
站着。掌櫃便自去了；晚上回來，說棺木須得現做，
後半夜纔成功。

　　掌櫃回來的時候，幫忙的人早喫過飯；因爲魯鎮
還有些古風，所以不上一更，便都回家睡覺了。只有
阿五還靠着咸亨的櫃臺喝酒，老拱也嗚嗚的唱。

　　這時候，單四嫂子坐在牀沿上哭着，寶兒在牀上
躺着，紡車靜靜的在地上立着。許多工夫，單四嫂子
的眼淚宣告完結了，眼睛張得很大，看看四面的情形，
覺得奇怪：所有的都是不會有的事。他心裏計算：不
過是夢罷了，這些事都是夢。明天醒過來，自己好好
的睡在牀上，寶兒也好好的睡在自己身邊。他也醒過
來，叫一聲『媽』，生龍活虎似的跳去玩了。

　　老拱的歌聲早經寂靜，咸亨也熄了燈。單四嫂子
張着眼，總不信所有的事。——雞也叫了；東方漸漸
發白，窗縫裏透進了銀白色的曙光。

　　銀白的曙光又漸漸顯出緋紅，太陽光接着照到屋
脊。單四嫂子張着眼，呆呆坐着；聽得打門聲音，纔

作抵	zuò dǐ	as security
棺木	guānmù	coffin
耳環	ěrhuán	ear-ring
裹金	guǒjīn	gold-plated
銀簪	yín zān	silver hair-pin
保	bǎo	surety
半現半賒	bàn xiàn bàn shē	half paid in cash, half on credit
自告奮勇	zǐ gào fènyǒng	to volunteer
差使	chāishǐ	errand, commission
怏怏	yàngyàng	unhappy
現做	xiàn zuò	to be made there and then
宣告	xuāngào	to declare (itself), to proclaim
完結	wánjié	to come to an end
生龍活虎	shēng lóng huó hǔ	full of life
東方發白	dōngfāng fā bái	light of dawn appearing in the east

喫了一嚇，跑出去開門。門外一個不認識的人，背了一件東西；後面站着王九媽。

哦，他們背了棺材來了。

下半天，棺木纔合上蓋：因爲單四嫂子哭一回，看一回，總不肯死心塌地的蓋上；幸虧王九媽等得不耐煩，氣憤憤的跑上前，一把拖開他，纔七手八脚的蓋上了。

但單四嫂子待他的寶兒，實在已經盡了心，再沒有什麼缺陷。昨天燒過一串紙錢。上午又燒了四十九卷《大悲咒》；收斂的時候，給他穿上頂新的衣裳，平日喜歡的玩意兒，——一個泥人，兩個小木碗，兩個玻璃瓶，——都放在枕頭旁邊。後來王九媽掐着指頭仔細推敲，也終于想不出一些什麼缺掐。

這一日裏，藍皮阿五簡直整天沒有到；咸亨掌櫃便替單四嫂子僱了兩名脚夫，每名二百另十個大錢，擡棺木到義塚地上安放。王九媽又幫他煮了飯，凡是動過手開過口的人都喫了飯。太陽漸漸顯出要落山的顏色；喫過飯的人也不覺都顯出要回家的顏色，——于是他們終于都回了家。

單四嫂子很覺得頭眩，歇息了一會，倒居然有點平穩了。但他接連着便覺得很異樣：遇到了平生沒有遇到過的事，不像會有的事，然而的確出現了。他越想越奇，又感到一件異樣的事：——這屋子忽然太靜了。

他站起身，點上燈火，屋子越顯得靜。他昏昏的

死心塌地	sǐ xīn tā dì	to reconcile oneself to one's situation, having given up all hope
七手八脚	qī shǒu bā jiǎo	descriptive of confused activity when everyone is trying to help
待	dài	to treat
盡了心	jìn le xīn	done everything possible
缺陷	qüēxiàn	defect, deficiency, something left undone (cf. 缺憾 qüē hàn)
串	chuàn	a string of
卷	jüàn	scroll – units into which a book is divided
大悲咒	dà bēi zhòu	a Buddhist incantation
收敛 (殮)	shōu liàn	to encoffin
頂 (最)	dǐng (zuì)	most
玩意兒	wányìr	toy (pl. here)
玻璃	bōlí	glass
招着指頭	qiā zhe zhǐ tóu	to do calculations on one's fingers
推敲	tuīqiāo	to go into a problem carefully
簡直	jiǎnzhí	practically
僱	gù	to hire
脚夫	jiǎofū	porter
另 (零)	líng	and (used between higher and lower figures in a single number)
義塚	yìzhǒng	grave for paupers and, more generally anyone for whom no one is responsible
頭眩	tóuxüàn	dizzy
異樣	yìyàng	strange, unfamiliar looking
平生	píngshēng	all one's life
的確	díqüè	undeniably, certainly
越…越…	yüè … yüè …	the more … the more …
昏昏	hūn hūn	in a daze

走去關上門，回來坐在牀沿上，紡車靜靜的立在地上。
他定一定神，四面一看，更覺得坐立不得，屋子不但
太靜，而且也太大了，東西也太空了，太大的屋子四
面包圍着他，太空的東西四面壓着他，叫他喘氣不得。

　　他現在知道他的寶兒確乎死了；不願意見這屋子，
吹熄了燈，躺着。他一面哭，一面想：想那時候，自
己紡着棉紗，寶兒坐在身邊喫茴香豆，瞪着一雙小黑
眼睛想了一刻，便說，『媽！爹賣餛飩，我大了也賣
餛飩，賣許多許多錢，——我都給你。』那時候，眞
是連紡出的棉紗，也彷彿寸寸都有意思，寸寸都活着。
但現在怎麼了？現在的事，單四嫂子卻實在沒有想到
什麼。——我早經說過：他是粗笨女人。他能想出什
麼呢？他單覺得這屋子太靜，太大，太空罷了。

　　但單四嫂子雖然粗笨，卻知道還魂是不能有的事，
他的寶兒也的確不能再見了。歎一口氣，自言自語的
說，『寶兒，你該還在這里，你給我夢裏見見罷。』
于是合上眼，想趕快睡去，會他的寶兒，苦苦的呼吸
通過了靜和大和空虛，自己聽得明白。

　　單四嫂子終于朦朦朧朧的走入睡鄉，全屋子都很
靜。這時紅鼻子老拱的小曲，也早經唱完；蹌蹌跟跟
出了咸亨，卻又提尖了喉嚨，唱道：——

　　『我的冤家呀！——可憐你，——孤另另的……』

　　藍皮阿五便伸手揪住了老拱的肩頭，兩個人七歪
八斜的笑着擠着走去。

　　單四嫂子早睡着了，老拱們也走了，咸亨也關上

坐立不得	zuò lǐ bù dé	restless, unable to remain sitting yet unable to remain standing
包圍	bāowéi	to ring in, completely surround
喘氣不得	chuǎn qì bù dé	unable to breathe, unable to get one's breath
確乎	qüèhū	certainly (hu class. adverbial suffix)
躺	tǎng	to lie (down)
瞪着	dèng zhe	with eyes wide open
餛飩	húntūn	a kind of meat-filled dumpling
還魂	huánhún	to come back to life again
空虛	kōngxū	void, emptiness
入睡鄉	rù shuìxiāng	to enter the land of sleep, to fall asleep
尖	jiān	sharp, shrill
孤另另（伶伶）	gūlínglíng	all alone in the world
揪	jiū	to grab hold of
七歪八斜	qī wāi bā xié	crooked, all over the place
擠	jǐ	to push against, to crowd, to jostle

門了。這時的魯鎭，便完全落在寂靜裏。只有那暗夜
爲想變成明天，卻仍在這寂靜裏奔波；另有幾條狗，
也躲在暗地裏嗚嗚的叫。

奔波	bēnbō	busy rushing here and there, working away

一件小事

　　我從鄉下跑到京城裏，一轉眼已經六年了。其間耳聞目覩的所謂國家大事，算起來也很不少；但在我心裏，都不留什麼痕迹，倘要我尋出這些事的影響來說，便只是增長了我的壞脾氣，——老實說，便是教我一天比一天的看不起人。

　　但有一件小事，卻于我有意義，將我從壞脾氣裏拖開，使我至今忘記不得。

　　這是民國六年的冬天，大北風刮得正猛，我因爲生計關係，不得不一早在路上走。一路幾乎遇不見人，好容易纔僱定了一輛人力車，教他拉到S門去。不一會，北風小了，路上浮塵早已刮淨，剩下一條潔白的大道來，車夫也跑得更快。剛近S門，忽而車把上帶着一個人，慢慢地倒了。

　　跌倒的是一個女人，花白頭髮，衣服都很破爛。伊從馬路邊上突然向車前橫截過來；車夫已經讓開道，但伊的破棉背心沒有上釦，微風吹着，向外展開，所以終于兜着車把。幸而車夫早有點停步，否則伊定要栽一個大斛斗，跌到頭破血出了。

　　伊伏在地上；車夫便也立住脚。我料定這老女人並沒有傷，又沒有別人看見，便很怪他多事，要自己

一件小事　Yí jiàn xiǎo shǐ

跑到	pǎo dào	to go all the way to
一轉眼	yì zhuǎn yǎn	in a twinkle
其間	qíjiàn	during that time
耳聞目覩	ěr wén mù dǔ	to have seen with one's own eyes and heard with one's own ears
國家大事	guójiā dà shǐ	important affairs of state, events of national importance
算起來	suàn qǐ lái	come to think of it
痕迹	hénjī	traces
倘	tǎng	if (supposition) (＝儻)
影響	yǐngxiǎng	effect, influence
增長	zēngzhǎng	to strengthen, to swell
老實說	lǎoshí shuō	to tell the truth, frankly speaking
看不起人	kàn bù qǐ rén	to look down on people
有意義	yǒu yìyì	significant
拖開	tuō kāi	to drag away from
刮得正猛	guā dé zhēng měng	was just at that moment blowing hard
因爲⋯關係	yìn wèi . . . guānxì	for the sake of, in connection with
生計	shēngjì	livelihood
好容易	hǎo róngyì	with the utmost difficulty
人力車	rénlì chē	(jin) ricksha(w) [the characters in Japanese pronunciation]
浮塵	fú chén	loose dust
刮淨	guā jìng	blown all away
車把	chēbǎ	the handle of the ricksha
帶	dài	to catch
跌倒	diē dǎo	to fall over
突然	tūrán	suddenly, abruptly, without warning
橫截	héng jié	to cut across
讓道	ràng dào	to get out of the way (to let another pass)
背心	bèixīn	sleeveless garment
上扣	shàngkòu	to do up the button
展開	zhǎn kāi	to spread out
兜着	dōu zhe	to wrap round
否則	fǒuzé	otherwise
栽一個觔斗	zāi yí gè jīndǒu	to turn a somersault
料定	liàodìng	to anticipate with certainty
怪	guài	to be displeased with someone (either for failing to do what he ought to do, or doing what he ought not to do)
多事	duōshì	officious, doing what is strictly unnecessary

惹出是非，也誤了我的路。

　　我便對他說，『沒有什麼的。走你的罷！』

　　車夫毫不理會，·──或者並沒有聽到，──卻放下車子，扶那老女人慢慢起來，攙着臂膊立定，問伊說：

　　『你怎麼啦？』

　　『我摔壞了。』

　　我想，我眼見你慢慢倒地，怎麼會摔壞呢，裝腔作勢罷了，這眞可憎惡。車夫多事，也正是自討苦喫，現在你自己想法去。

　　車夫聽了這老女人的話，卻毫不躊躕，仍然攙着伊的臂膊，便一步一步的向前走。我有些詫異，忙看前面，是一所巡警分駐所，大風之後，外面也不見人。這車夫扶着那老女人，便正是向那大門走去。

　　我這時突然感到一種異樣的感覺，覺得他滿身灰塵的後影，刹時高大了，而且愈走愈大，須仰視纔見。而且他對于我，漸漸的又幾乎變成一種威壓，甚而至于要搾出皮袍下面藏着的『小』來。

　　我的活力這時大約有些凝滯了，坐着沒有動，也沒有想，直到看見分駐所裏走出一個巡警，纔下了車。

　　巡警走近我說，『你自己僱車罷，他不能拉你了。』

　　我沒有思索的從外套袋裏抓出一大把銅元，交給巡警，說，『請你給他……』

　　風全住了，路上還很靜。我走着，一面想，幾乎怕敢想到我自己。以前的事姑且擱起，這一大把銅元

惹出是非	rě chū shìfēi	to land (someone or oneself) in trouble
誤	wù	to cause to delay
走你的罷	zǒu nǐ de bà	be on your way
毫	háo	in the least (followed by negative)
理會	lǐhuì	to pay attention
或者	huòzhě	perhaps
卻	qüè	instead, on the contrary
攙	cān	to support by holding someone up
立定	lì dìng	to stand still, to gain a firm footing
摔壞	shuāi huài	to be hurt in the fall
裝腔作勢	zhuāng qiāng zuò shì	to put it all on
可憎惡	kě zēngwù	detestable
自討苦喫	zì tǎo kǔ chī	to ask for trouble
詫異	chàyì	surprised
巡警	xúnjǐng	policeman
分駐所	fēn zhù suǒ	post
後影	hòu yǐng	rear view
利（霎）時	shà shí	in a moment, suddenly
仰視	yǎng shì	to look up
威壓	wēi yā	threateningly oppressive
搾出	zhà chū	squeeze out
皮袍	pí páo	fur coat
活力	huólì	vitality, élan
凝滯	níngzhì	congealed, no longer freely circulating
僱	gù	to hire
思索	sīsuǒ	to think; to turn a problem over in one's mind
一大把	yí dà bǎ	a large handful
姑且	gūqiě	for the time being (suggesting an action that is tentative)
擱	gē	to put aside

又是什麼意思？獎他麼？我還能裁判車夫麼？我不能
回答自己。

　　這事到了現在，還是時時記起。我因此也時時熬
了苦痛，努力的要想到我自己。幾年來的文治武力，
在我早如幼小時候所讀過的『子曰詩云』一般，背不
上半句了。獨有這一件小事，卻總是浮在我眼前，有
時反更分明，教我慚愧，催我自新，並且增長我的勇
氣和希望。

獎	jiǎng	to reward, to encourage
裁判	cáipàn	to pass (legal) judgement on
熬	aó	to undergo suffering; to stew
努力的	nǔlì de	to try hard to
文治武力	wén zhì wǔ lì	successes in government or in war
子曰詩云	zǐ yüē shì yún	the Master said (referring to the *Analects of Confucius*), the Poem has it (referring to the *Book of Poetry*), hence the classics
背	bèi	to repeat by rote
分明	fēnmíng	distinct
慚愧	cánkuì	ashamed
催	cuī	to urge, to hasten
自新	zì xīn	to renew oneself, to turn a new page
勇氣	yǒngqì	courage
希望	xīwàng	hope

頭髮的故事

　　星期日的早晨，我揭去一張隔夜的日曆，向着新的那一張上看了又看的說：

　　『阿，十月十日，──今天原來正是雙十節。這里卻一點沒有記載！』

　　我的一位前輩先生N，正走到我的寓裏來談閒天，一聽這話，便很不高興的對我說：

　　『他們對！他們不記得，你怎樣他；你記得，又怎樣呢！』

　　這位N先生本來脾氣有點乖張，時常生些無謂的氣，說些不通世故的話。當這時候，我大抵任他自言自語，不贊一辭；他獨自發完議論，也就算了。

　　他說：

　　『我最佩服北京雙十節的情形。早晨，警察到門，吩咐道「掛旗！」「是，掛旗！」各家大半懶洋洋的踱出一個國民來，撅起一塊斑駁陸離的洋布。這樣一直到夜，──收了旗關門；幾家偶然忘卻的，便掛到第二天的上午。

　　他們忘卻了紀念，紀念也忘卻了他們！

　　我也是忘卻了紀念的一個人。倘使紀念起來，那第一個雙十節前後的事，便都上我的心頭，使我坐立不穩了。

頭髮的故事　Tóufà de gùshì

揭去	jiēqù	to lift off, to tear off
隔夜	géyè	overnight, left over from the previous night
日曆	rìlì	calendar, here pages of the calendar
正是	zhèngshì	precisely, exactly to be
雙十節	shuāngshí jié	Double Ten : October 10th
記載	jìzǎi	to note, to record
前輩	qiánbèi	one's senior
你怎樣他	ní zěn yàng tā	what can you do about it?
又怎樣呢	yòu zěn yàng ne	so what?
乖張	guāizhāng	perverse
無謂	wúwèi	pointless, to no purpose at all
生氣	shēng qì	to get angry
不通世故	bù tōng shìgù	ignorant of the ways of the world
大抵	dàdǐ	generally speaking
任	rèn	to let, to allow
不贊一辭	bú zàn yì cí	not to put in a word
發議論	fā yìlùn	to hold forth
也就算了	yě jiù suàn lě	to let it pass
佩服	pèifú	to admire someone's superiority
吩咐	fēnfù	to give instructions what to do
懶洋洋的	lǎnyángyáng de	lethargically
踱	duò	to walk slowly or deliberately
國民	guómín	citizen
撅起	jüē qǐ	to stick up (e.g. animal sticking up its tail)
斑駁陸離	bān bó lù lí	variegated
洋	yáng	foreign
前後	qiánhòu	round about
上心頭	shàng xīntóu	to well up in the mind
坐立不穩	zuò lì bù wěn	uneasy, fidgety

　　多少故人的臉，都浮在我眼前。幾個少年辛苦奔走
了十多年，暗地裏一顆彈丸要了他的性命；幾個少年
一擊不中，在監牢裏身受一個多月的苦刑；幾個少年懷
着遠志，忽然蹤影全無，連屍首也不知那里去了。——

　　他們都在社會的冷笑惡罵迫害傾陷裏過了一生；
現在他們的墳墓也早在忘卻裏漸漸平塌下去了。

　　我不堪紀念這些事。

　　我們還是記起一點得意的事來談談罷。』

　　Ｎ忽然現出笑容，伸手在自己頭上一摸，高聲說：

　　『我最得意的是自從第一個雙十節以後，我在路
上走，不再被人笑罵了。

　　老兄，你可知道頭髮是我們中國人的寶貝和冤家，
古今來多少人在這上頭喫些毫無價值的苦呵！

　　我們的很古的古人，對於頭髮似乎也還看輕。據
刑法看來，最要緊的自然是腦袋，所以大辟是上刑；
次要便是生殖器了，所以宮刑和幽閉也是一件嚇人的
罰；至于髡，那是微乎其微了；然而推想起來，正不
知道曾有多少人們因爲光着頭皮便被社會踐踏了一生
世。

　　我們講革命的時候，大談什麼揚州十日，嘉定屠
城，其實也不過一種手段；老實說：那時中國人的反
抗，何嘗因爲亡國，只是因爲拖辮子。

　　頑民殺盡了，遺老都壽終了，辮子早留定了，洪
楊又鬧起來了。我的祖母曾對我說，那時做百姓纔難

故人	gùrén	old friends
辛苦	xīnkǔ	hardship
奔走	bēnzǒu	to wear oneself out in the services of
暗地裡	àndìlǐ	on the quiet
一顆彈丸	yì kē dànwán	a bullet
要了性命	yào le xìngmìng	taken (someone's) life
監牢	jiānláo	gaol
苦刑	kǔ xíng	cruel torture
懷着遠志	huái zhe yüǎn zhì	to cherish great ambition
蹤影全無	zōngyǐng qüán wú	without trace
屍首	shīshǒu	body, i.e., corpse
惡罵	è mà	cruel curses
迫害	pòhài	persecution
傾陷	qīngxiàn	attempt to get someone into trouble
平塌	píngtā	to subside, to flatten
不堪	bùkān	unable to bear
得意	déyì	to be proud of (e.g., success, achievement)
寶貝	bǎobèi	treasured object (also used of persons)
冤家	yüānjiā	implacable enemy
古今來	gǔ jīn lái	down the ages
在這上頭	zài zhè shàngtóu	on this score
還	hái	as yet
刑法	xíngfǎ	penal code
腦袋	nǎodài	head
大辟	dàpì	capital punishment (lit.)
生殖器	shēngzhí qì	sex organ
宮刑	gōng xíng	castration
幽閉	yōubì	punishment of women by removal of ovaries
嚇人	xiàrén	frightening
髡	kūn	punishment by shaving off the hair
微乎其微	wēi hū qí wēi	insignificant of the insignificant
推想	tuīxiǎng	to infer, to think more about it
光着頭皮	guāng zhe tóupí	with a bald head
踐踏	jiàntà	to stamp upon, to tread upon
一生世	yì shēng shì	a lifetime
楊州十日	YángZhōu shí rì	the ten days of Yangchou
嘉定屠城	JiāDìng tú chéng	the massacre of the city of Chiating (both refer to accounts of the massacres carried out by the Manchu army when they conquered China)
手段	shǒuduàn	a means
反抗	fǎnkàng	resistance
何嘗	hécháng	not at all
頑民	wánmín	incorrigible rebels
遺老	yílào	surviving officials from a previous dynasty
壽終	shòuzhōng	to die of old age
洪楊	Hóng Yáng	Hong Xiu-qüan 洪秀全 and Yang Xiu-qing 楊秀清, both leaders of the Tai-pings

哩，全留着頭髮的被官兵殺，還是辮子的便被長毛殺！

　　我不知道有多少中國人只因爲這不痛不癢的頭髮而喫苦，受難，滅亡。』

　　N 兩眼望着屋梁，似乎想些事，仍然説：

　　『誰知道頭髮的苦輪到我了。

　　我出去留學，便剪掉了辮子，這並沒有別的奧妙，只爲他太不便當罷了。不料有幾位辮子盤在頭頂上的同學們便很厭惡我；監督也大怒，説要停了我的官費，送回中國去。

　　不幾天，這位監督卻自己被人剪去辮子逃走了。去剪的人們裏面，一個便是做《革命軍》的鄒容，這人也因此不能再留學，回到上海來，後來死在西牢裏。你也早已忘卻了罷。

　　過了幾年，我的家景大不如前了，非謀點事做便要受餓，只得也回到中國來。我一到上海，便買定一條假辮子，那時是二元的市價，帶着回家。我的母親倒也不説什麽，然而旁人一見面，便都首先研究這辮子，待到知道是假，就一聲冷笑，將我擬爲殺頭的罪名；有一位本家，還豫備去告官，但後來因爲恐怕革命黨的造反或者要成功，這纔中止了。

　　我想，假的不如眞的直截爽快，我便索性廢了假辮了，穿着西裝在街上走。

　　一路走去，一路便是笑罵的聲音，有的還跟在後面罵：「這冒失鬼！」「假洋鬼子！」

　　我于是不穿洋服了，改了大衫，他們罵得更利害。

長毛	chángmáo	the Taipings
不痛不癢	bú tòng bù yǎng	of no importance at all
受難	shòu nàn	to go through ordeal
屋梁	wū liáng	a beam
輪到我	lún dào wǒ	my turn came
留學	liúxüé	to study abroad
剪掉	jiǎn diào	to cut off
奧妙	aòmiào	mystery
便當（方便）	biàn dàng	convenient
不料	bú liào	I never thought
盤	pán	to coil
厭惡	yànwù	to detest
監督	jiāndū	supervisor
官費	guān fèi	government grant
西牢	xī láo	name of a gaol
家景	jiājǐng	family circumstances
謀事	móu shì	to look for a job
市價	shì jià	current price
待到	dài dào	by the time
冷笑	lěngxiào	to sneer
擬	nǐ	to submit proposal to higher authority, to make a draft
中止	zhōngzhǐ	to give up (action) half way
直截爽快	zhí jié shuǎngkuài	straightforward and not in a round-about manner
索性	suǒxìng	to go the whole hog, might as well
廢	fèi	to get rid of
西裝	xīzhuāng	Western style clothes
冒失鬼	màoshi guǐ	reckless fellow
假洋鬼子	jiǎ yáng guǐz	imitation foreign devil
大衫	dàshān	a long jacket

　　在這日暮途窮的時候，我的手裏纔添出一支手杖來，拚命的打了幾回，他們漸漸的不罵了。只是走到沒有打過的生地方還是罵。

　　這件事很使我悲哀，至今還時時記得哩。我在留學的時候，曾經看見日報上登載一個游歷南洋和中國的本多博士的事；這位博士是不懂中國和馬來語的，人問他，你不懂話，怎麼走路呢？他拿起手杖來說，這便是他們的話，他們都懂！我因此氣憤了好幾天，誰知道我竟不知不覺的自己也做了，而且那些人都懂了。……

　　宣統初年，我在本地的中學校做監學，同事是避之惟恐不遠，官僚是防之惟恐不嚴，我終日如坐在冰窖子裏，如站在刑場旁邊，其實並非別的，只因爲缺少了一條辮子！

　　有一日，幾個學生忽然走到我的房裏來，說，「先生，我們要剪辮子了。」我說，「不行！」「有辮子好呢，沒有辮子好呢？」「沒有辮子好……」「你怎麼說不行呢？」「犯不上，你們還是不剪上算，——等一等罷。」他們不說什麼，撅着嘴唇走出房去；然而終于剪掉了。

　　呵！不得了了，人言嘖嘖了；我卻只裝作不知道，一任他們光着頭皮，和許多辮子一齊上講堂。

　　然而這剪辮病傳染了；第三天，師範學堂的學生忽然也剪下了六條辮子，晚上便開除了六個學生。這六個人，留校不能，回家不得，一直挨到第一個雙十

日暮途窮	rì mù tú qióng	the end of the road, with nowhere to turn to
添	tiān	with something added to, to have an extra something
手杖	shǒuzhàng	walking stick
拚命	pànmìng	with all one's might
生地方	shēng dìfāng	strange, unfamiliar place
日報	rìbào	a daily
登載	dēngzài	to carry on its pages
游歷	yóulì	tour
南洋	Nán Yáng	the Malaysian region
博士	bóshì	holder of a doctorate
不知不覺	bù zhī bù jüé	imperceptibly (referring to gradual change)
宣統	Xüān Tǒng	reign period of last Ch'ing emperor (1909 – 1911)
監學	jiānxüé	school superintendent
同事	tóngshì	colleague
避之唯恐不遠	bì zhī wéi kǒng bù yüǎn	(class.) could not give me a wide enough berth
官僚	guānliáo	bureaucrats
防之唯恐不嚴	fáng zhī wéi kong bù yǎn	could not keep too strict an eye on me
冰窖子	bìng gàoz	ice-house
並非別的	bìng fēi bié de	was for no other reason than
缺	qüē	to lack
犯不上	fàn bú shàng	not worth it
上算	shàng suàn	a better course of action
撅着嘴唇	jüē zhe zuǐchún	to pout
不得了	bù de liǎo	it was awful
人言嘖嘖	rén yán zé zé	there was a lot of talk
裝作	zhuāng zuò	to pretend
講堂	jiǎngtáng	lecture hall, classroom
傳染	chuánrǎn	to infect
師範學堂	shīfàn xüétáng	normal college, teachers' training college
開除	kāichú	to send down, to sack
挨（捱）	aí	to go through (trying period of time), to put up with

節之後又一個多月，纔消去了犯罪的火烙印。

　　我呢？也一樣，只是元年冬天到北京，還被人罵過幾次，後來罵我的人也被警察剪去了辮子，我就不再被人辱罵了；但我沒有到鄉間去。』

　　N 顯出非常得意模樣，忽而又沈下臉來：

　　『現在你們這些理想家，又在那里嚷什麼女子剪髮了，又要造出許多毫無所得而痛苦的人！

　　現在不是已經有剪掉頭髮的女人，因此考不進學校去，或者被學校除了名麼？

　　改革麼，武器在那里？工讀麼，工廠在那里？

　　仍然留起，嫁給人家做媳婦去：忘卻了一切還是幸福，倘使伊記着些平等自由的話，便要苦痛一生世！

　　我要借了阿爾志跋綏夫的話問你們：你們將黃金時代的出現豫約給這些人們的子孫了，但有什麼給這些人們自己呢？

　　阿，造物的皮鞭沒有到中國的脊梁上時，中國便永遠是這一樣的中國，決不肯自己改變一支毫毛！

　　你們的嘴裏旣然並無毒牙，何以偏要在額上帖起「蝮蛇」兩個大字，引乞丐來打殺？……』

　　N 愈說愈離奇了，但一見到我不很願聽的神情，便立刻閉了口，站起來取帽子。

　　我說，『回去麼？』

　　他答道，『是的，天要下雨了。』

　　我默默的送他到門口。

　　他戴上帽子說：

火烙印	huǒ lào yìn	the mark of branding
元年	yüán nián	the first year (here of the Republic)
沈下臉來	chén xià liǎn lái	suddenly to put on a severe countenance; to turn nasty
理想家	líxiǎng jiā	idealists
毫無所得	háo wú suǒ dé	to have gained nothing at all
考不進	kǎo bú jìn	to fail the entrance examination
除了名	chú le míng	struck off the register
改革	gǎigé	to reform [Lu Xün is here deliberately avoiding the word 革命 in order not to get into trouble with the authorities]
武器	wǔqì	weapons
工讀	gōngdú	to work through college
工廠	gōngchǎng	factory
留起	liú qǐ	to grow (hair) long
媳婦	xífù	wife; daughter-in-law
平等自由	píngděng zìyóu	equality, liberty
豫約	yùyüē	prepayment for a book before publication, subscribe for a book
造物	zaòwù	Creator
皮鞭	pí biān	whip
毫毛	háomáo	a hair
毒牙	dú yá	poisoned fangs
蝮蛇	fù shé	venomous snake
乞丐	qǐgài	beggars (In popular tradition beggars are credited with special skill in dealing with snakes)
離奇	líqí	extraordinary
默默的	mòmò de	silently

　　『再見！請你恕我打攪，好在明天便不是雙十節，我們統可以忘卻了。』

| 打攪 | dǎjiǎo | to disturb |
| 統 | tǒng | completely |

風波

　　臨河的土場上，太陽漸漸的收了他通黃的光線了。場邊靠河的烏桕樹葉，乾巴巴的纔喘過氣來，幾個花腳蚊子在下面哼着飛舞。面河的農家的煙突裏，逐漸減少了炊煙，女人孩子們都在自己門口的土場上潑些水，放下小桌子和矮凳；人知道，這已經是晚飯時候了。

　　老人男人坐在矮凳上，搖着大芭蕉扇閒談，孩子飛也似的跑，或者蹲在烏桕樹下賭玩石子。女人端出烏黑的蒸乾菜和松花黃的米飯，熱蓬蓬冒煙。河裏駛過文人的酒船，文豪見了，大發詩興，說，『無思無慮，這真是田家樂呵！』

　　但文豪的話有些不合事實，就因為他們沒有聽到九斤老太的話。這時候，九斤老太正在大怒，拿破芭蕉扇敲着凳脚說：

　　『我活到七十九歲了，活夠了，不願意眼見這些敗家相，──還是死的好。立刻就要喫飯了，還喫炒豆子，喫窮了一家子！』

　　伊的曾孫女兒六斤捏着一把豆，正從對面跑來，見這情形，便直奔河邊，藏在烏桕樹後，伸出雙丫角

風波　Fēng bō

臨	lín	to overlook, to be on the verge of, to be faced with
土場	tǔcháng	open space with mud surface, mud yard
通	tōng	(pref.) through and through, all over
通黃	tōng huáng	yellow right through
烏桕	wūjiù	tallow tree
乾巴巴的	gānbā bā de	dried, parched
纔喘過氣來	cái chuǎn guò qì lái	had just got its breath back
哼着	hēng je	humming
面河	miàn hé	facing the river
煙突	yāntū	chimney
逐漸	zhújiàn	gradually, little by little
減少	jiǎnshǎo	to decrease
炊煙	chūiyān	smoke from cooking
潑	pō	to throw water out, to splash
矮凳	ǎi dèng	low stool
搖	yáo	to wave
芭蕉扇	bājiāo shàn	plantain leaf fan
閒談	xiántan	to chat
蹲	dūn	to squat
賭	dǔ	to wager, to play a game
烏黑	wūhēi	jet black
蒸	zhēng	to steam
乾菜	gān cài	dried vegetable
松花黃	sōnghuā huáng	the yellow colour of pine flowers
熱蓬蓬	rèpéngpéng	steaming hot
煙	yān	smoke, but *also* steam, haze etc.
駛	shǐ	to steer a boat or a vehicle, hence to sail, to drive
文人	wénrén	literary men
文豪	wénháo	famous author
發詩興	fā shī xìng	bursting with urge to write poetry
無思無慮	wú sī wú lù	without a care in the world
田家樂	tiánjiā lè	idyllic happiness
事實	shìshí	facts, what is actually the case, what actually happened
敲	qiāo	to knock on
敗家	bàijiā	to ruin the family fortune
相	xiàng	the looks, signs
曾孫女兒	zēng sūn nǚ ér	great-grand-daughter
捏着	niē je	clutching
直奔	zhí bēn	to make straight for

的小頭，大聲說，『這老不死的！』

　　九斤老太雖然高壽，耳朶卻還不很聾，但也沒有聽到孩子的話，仍舊自己說，『這眞是一代不如一代！』

　　這村莊的習慣有點特別，女人生下孩子，多喜歡用秤稱了輕重，便用斤數當作小名。九斤老太自從慶祝了五十大壽以後，便漸漸的變了不平家，常說伊年靑的時候，天氣沒有現在這般熱，豆子也沒有現在這般硬：總之現在的時世是不對了。何況六斤比伊的曾祖，少了三斤，比伊父親七斤，又少了一斤，這眞是一條顚撲不破的實例。所以伊又用勁說，『這眞是一代不如一代！』

　　伊的兒媳七斤嫂子正捧着飯籃走到桌邊，便將飯籃在桌上一摔，憤憤的說，『你老人家又這麼說了。六斤生下來的時候，不是六斤五兩麼？你家的秤又是私秤，加重稱，十八兩秤；用了準十六，我們的六斤該有七斤多哩。我想便是太公和公公，也不見得正是九斤八斤十足，用的秤也許是十四兩……』

　　『一代不如一代！』

　　七斤嫂還沒有答話，忽然看見七斤從小巷口轉出，便移了方向，對他嚷道，『你這死屍怎麼這時候纔回來，死到那里去了！不管人家等着你開飯！』

　　七斤雖然住在農村，卻早有些飛黃騰達的意思。從他的祖父到他，三代不捏鋤頭柄了；他也照例的幫人撐着航船，每日一回，早晨從魯鎭進城，傍晚又回到魯鎭，因此很知道些時事：例如什麼地方，雷公劈

雙丫角	shuāng yājiǎo	a pair of short pigtails sticking out on either side of the head
老不死	lǎo bù sǐ	abusive term: one should have been dead long ago
高壽	gāoshòu	ripe old age
村莊	cūnzhuāng	village
特別	tèbié	unusual, peculiar
秤	chèng	steelyard
稱	chēng	to weigh (cogn. with previous word)
輕重	qīngzhòng	weight
小名	xiǎomíng	pet name
慶祝	qìngzhù	to celebrate
大壽（壽）	dàshòu	important birthday
不平家	bùpíng jiā	a grouser (Jap. expression)
時世	shíshì	the age, the times
顛撲不破	diānpū bú pò	having stood the test of time, unbreakable
實例	shí lì	actual example, here formula
兒媳	érxí	daughter-in-law
摔	shuāi	to throw down, to plonk down
私秤	sī chèng	private, i.e. non-standard, steelyard
準	zhǔn	accurate, exact
十足	shízú	fully (ref. primarily to quantities)
死屍	sǐshī	cadaver
死	sǐ	an abusive word used in the place where a verb ought to be
不管	bù guǎn	not caring
飛黃騰達	fēihuáng téng dá	to be very successful (in one's official career)
照例	zhào lì	as is the rule
撐	chēng	to pole a boat
航船	háng chuán	a boat on a regular service
傍晚	bàng wǎn	evening
時事	shíshì	what is happening in the world; current affairs
例如	lì rú	for example
雷公	léigōng	the thunder god
劈	pī	to strike

死了蜈蚣精；什麼地方，閨女生了一個夜叉之類。他在村人裏面，的確已經是一名出場人物了。但夏天喫飯不點燈，卻還守着農家習慣，所以回家太遲，是該罵的。

七斤一手捏着象牙嘴白銅斗六尺多長的湘妃竹煙管，低着頭，慢慢地走來，坐在矮凳上。六斤也趁勢溜出，坐在他身邊，叫他爹爹。七斤沒有應。

『一代不如一代！』九斤老太說。

七斤慢慢地擡起頭來，歎一口氣說，『皇帝坐了龍庭了。』

七斤嫂呆了一刻，忽而恍然大悟的道，『這可好了，這不是又要皇恩大赦了麼！』

七斤又歎一口氣，說，『我沒有辮子。』

『皇帝要辮子麼？』

『皇帝要辮子。』

『你怎麼知道呢？』七斤嫂有些着急，趕忙的問。

『咸亨酒店裏的人，都說要的。』

七斤嫂這時從直覺上覺得事情似乎有些不妙了，因爲咸亨酒店是消息靈通的所在。伊一轉眼瞥見七斤的光頭，便忍不住動怒，怪他恨他怨他；忽然又絕望起來，裝好一碗飯，搡在七斤的面前道，『還是趕快喫你的飯罷！哭喪着臉，就會長出辮子來麼？』

太陽收盡了他最末的光線了，水面暗暗地回復過涼氣來；土場上一片碗筷聲響，人人的脊梁上又都吐出汗粒。七斤嫂喫完三碗飯，偶然擡起頭，心坎裏便

蜈蚣	wúgōng	centipede
精	jīng	any object, e.g. an animal or a tree, which has acquired magical powers
閨女	guīnǚ	a girl who is as yet unmarried
夜叉	yèchā	a demon that harms humans [from Sanskrit yakṣa]
出場人物	chū chǎng rénwù	a figure in the public eye
白銅	báitóng	an alloy consisting of three parts of copper to one part of nickel
斗	dǒu	bowl
湘妃竹	xiāngfēi zhú	speckled bamboo
溜出	liū chū	to slip out
坐龍庭	zuò lóngtíng	to hold (royal) court
皇恩大赦	huáng ēn dà shè	a general amnesty by royal decree
直覺	zhíjué	intuition
不妙	bú miào	to bode ill
搡	sǎng	to push
哭喪着臉	kūsāng je liǎn	with a mournful face
心坎裏	xīnkǎn lǐ	the space in which the heart is

禁不住突突地發跳。伊透過烏桕葉，看見又矮又胖的
趙七爺正從獨木橋上走來，而且穿着寶藍色竹布的長
衫。

　　趙七爺是鄰村茂源酒店的主人，又是這三十里方
圓以內的唯一的出色人物兼學問家；因爲有學問，所
以又有些遺老的臭味。他有十多本金聖歎批評的《三
國志》，時常坐着一個字一個字的讀；他不但能說出
五虎將姓名，甚而至于還知道黃忠表字漢升和馬超表
字孟起。革命以後，他便將辮子盤在頂上，像道士一
般；常常歎息說，倘若趙子龍在世，天下便不會亂到
這地步了。七斤嫂眼睛好，早望見今天的趙七爺已經
不是道士，卻變成光滑頭皮，烏黑髮頂；伊便知道這
一定是皇帝坐了龍庭，而且一定須有辮子，而且七斤
一定是非常危險。因爲趙七爺的這件竹布長衫，輕易
是不常穿的，三年以來，只穿過兩次；一次是和他嘔
氣的麻子阿四病了的時候，一次是曾經砸爛他酒店的
魯大爺死了的時候；現在是第三次了，這一定又是于
他有慶，于他的仇家有殃了。

　　七斤嫂記得，兩年前七斤喝醉了酒，曾經罵過趙
七爺是『賤胎』，所以這時便立刻直覺到七斤的危險，
心坎裏突突地發起跳來。

　　趙七爺一路走來，坐着喫飯的人都站起身，拏筷
子點着自己的飯碗說，『七爺，請在我們這里用飯！』
七爺也一路點頭，說道『請請』，卻一徑走到七斤家
的桌旁。七斤們連忙招呼，七爺也微笑着說『請請』，

獨木橋	dúmù qiáo	a bridge consisting of a single log
寶藍	bǎolán	bright blue
竹布	zhúbù	cotton
…方圓	... fāngyüán	within an area of
出色	chūsè	distinguished
有…臭味	yǒu ... chòuwèi	to smack of
金聖歎	Jǐn Shèng Tàn	man of letters and critic put to death by the Manchus, c. 1610-61
批評	pīpíng	critical comments, criticism; to criticise
三國志 （演義）	Sān Guó Zhǐ (Yǎn Yì)	*Romance of the Three Kingdoms,* a fictionalised version of the *San Guo Zhi,* a history of the Three Kingdoms Period (220-265)
五虎將	Wú Hǔ Jiàng	five brave generals of the Kingdom of Shu
表字	biǎozì = 字 zi	the name used to address a man by people outside his family
歎息	tànxi	to sigh, to lament
地步	dìbù	extent, (come to such a) pass
道士	dàoshì	Taoist priest
光滑	guānghuá	shiny and smooth
輕易	qīngyì	lightly (used with negative)
嘔氣	òuqì	to quarrel
砸爛	zá làn	to smash up
慶，殃	qìng, yāng	(class.) good fortune, bad fortune
賤胎	jiàntāi	bastard
點	diǎn	dot, to dot, hence to touch (with tip of something)
用飯	yòng fàn	to have a meal (polite)
請請	qǐng qǐng	please carry on
連忙	líanmáng	to make haste (to do something)
招呼	zhāohu	to greet, to look after (guest, etc.)

一面細細的研究他們的飯菜。

　　『好香的乾菜，——聽到了風聲了麼？』趙七爺站在七斤的後面七斤嫂的對面說。

　　『皇帝坐了龍庭了。』七斤說。

　　七斤嫂看着七爺的臉，竭力陪笑道，『皇帝已經坐了龍庭，幾時皇恩大赦呢？』

　　『皇恩大赦？——大赦是慢慢的總要大赦罷。』七爺說到這里，聲色忽然嚴厲起來，『但是你家七斤的辮子呢，辮子？這倒是要緊的事。這們知道：長毛時候，留髮不留頭，留頭不留髮，……』

　　七斤和他的女人沒有讀過書，不很懂得這古典的奧妙，但覺得有學問的七爺這麼說，事情自然非常重大，無可挽回，便彷彿受了死刑宣告似的，耳朵裏嗡的一聲，再也說不出一句話。

　　『一代不如一代，——』九斤老太正在不平，趁這機會，便對趙七爺說，『現在的長毛，只是剪人家的辮子，僧不僧，道不道的。從前的長毛，這樣的麼？我活到七十九歲了，活夠了。從前的長毛是——整匹的紅緞子裹頭，拖下去，拖下去，一直拖到脚跟；王爺是黃緞子，拖下去，黃緞子，紅緞子，黃緞子，——我活夠了，七十九歲了。』

　　七斤嫂站起身，自言自語的說，『這怎麼好呢？這樣的一班老小，都靠他養活的人，……』

　　趙七爺搖頭道，『那也沒法。沒有辮子，該當何罪，書上都一條一條明明白白寫着的。不管他家裏有

研究	yánjiū	to study
風聲	fēngshēng	rumours, (to get) wind (of)
竭力	jiélì	to try one's utmost
陪笑	péishào	to smile apologetically or ingratiatingly
慢慢總要	mànmàn zǒng yào	bound to in due course
聲色	shēngsè	tone of voice and expression on face
嚴厲	yánlì	severe
古典	gǔdiǎn	allusion
奧妙	aòmiào	subtle and profound significance
重大	zhòngdà	grave
挽回	wǎnhúi	to save the situation, lit. to pull back from the brink (cf.挽救)
宣告	xüāngào	to pronounce, pronouncement, to proclaim
嗡	wēng	hum (onomat.)
a 不 a, b 不 b		neither the one thing nor the other
匹	pǐ	a roll of silk or cloth
裹	guǒ	to wrap round
拖	tuō	to trail, to drag
脚跟	jiǎogēn	heel
王爺	wángyé	a royal prince
緞	duàn	satin
一班	yì bān	whole lot of
該當何罪	gāi dāng hé zùi	(phrase in traditional novels) what penalty does this deserve?
一條	yì tiáo	an item

些什麼人。』

　　七斤嫂聽到書上寫着，可眞是完全絕望了；自己急得沒法，便忽然又恨到七斤。伊用筷子指着他的鼻尖說，『這死屍自作自受！造反的時候，我本來說，不要撐船了，不要上城了。他偏要死進城去，滾進城去，進城便被人剪去了辮子。從前是絹光烏黑的辮子，現在弄得僧不僧道不道的。這囚徒自作自受，帶累了我們又怎麼說呢？這活死屍的囚徒……』

　　村人看見趙七爺到村，都趕緊喫完飯，聚在七斤家飯桌的周圍。七斤自己知道是出場人物，被女人當大衆這樣辱罵，很不雅觀，便只得擡起頭，慢慢地說道：

　　　　『你今天說現成話，那時你……』

　　　　『你這活死屍的囚徒……』

　　看客中間，八一嫂是心腸最好的人，抱着伊的兩週歲的遺腹子，正在七斤嫂身邊看熱鬧；這時過意不去，連忙解勸說，『七斤嫂，算了罷。人不是神仙，誰知道未來事呢？便是七斤嫂，那時不也說，沒有辮子倒也沒有什麼醜麼？況且衙門裏的大老爺也還沒有告示，……』

　　七斤嫂沒有聽完，兩個耳朵早通紅了；便將筷子轉過向來，指着八一嫂的鼻子，說，『阿呀，這是什麼話呵！八一嫂，我自己看來倒還是一個人，會說出這樣昏誕胡塗話麼？那時我是，整整哭了三天，誰都看見；連六斤這小鬼也都哭，……』六斤剛喫完一大

自作自受	zì zuò zì shòu	to suffer what is one's own making
偏要	piānyào	to insist (out of contrariness)
滾	gǔn	to roll along, an abusive word used in place of verbs of motion
囚徒	qiútú	convict
帶累	dàilèi	to involve others in one's own trouble
趕緊	gǎnjǐn	to hasten to (do something)
當大衆	dāng dàzhòng	in front of everyone, in public
辱罵	rùmà	to curse and humiliate
不雅觀	bù yǎguān	unseemly
說現成話	shuō xiànchéng huà	to be wise after the event, it is easy for you to say so now
看客	kànkè	spectators
心腸好	xīncháng hǎo	kind-hearted
週歲	zhōusùi	fully a year old
遺腹子	yífùzǐ	a posthumous son
看熱鬧	kàn rè'nào	to watch the fun
過意不去	guò yì bú qù	to feel sorry for, to think it going too far, to feel badly about something
解勸	jiěqüàn	to placate
神仙	shénxiān	immortal, god
未來事	wèilái shì	future events
衙門	yámén	yamen
大老爺	dà lǎo yé	(referring to officials) (your, his) lordship
告示	gàoshì	notice
昏誕胡塗話	hūndàn hútú huà	nonsense

碗飯，挈了空碗，伸手去嚷着要添。七斤嫂正沒好氣，便用筷子在伊的雙丫角中間，直扎下去，大喝道，『誰要你來多嘴！你這偷漢的小寡婦！』

撲的一聲，六斤手裏的空碗落在地上了，恰巧又碰着一塊磚角，立刻破成一個很大的缺口。七斤直跳起來，檢起破碗，合上了檢查一回，也喝道，『入娘的！』一巴掌打倒了六斤。六斤躺着哭，九斤老太拉了伊的手，連說着『一代不如一代』，一同走了。

八一嫂也發怒，大聲說，『七斤嫂，你「恨棒打人」……』

趙七爺本來是笑着旁觀的；但自從八一嫂說了『衙門裏的大老爺沒有告示』這話以後，卻有些生氣了。這時他已經遶出桌旁，接着說，『「恨棒打人」，算什麼呢。大兵是就要到的。你可知道，這回保駕的是張大帥，張大帥就是燕人張翼德的後代，他一支丈八蛇矛，就有萬夫不當之勇，誰能抵擋他，』他兩手同時捏起空拳，彷彿握着無形的蛇矛模樣，向八一嫂搶進幾步道，『你能抵擋他麼！』

八一嫂正氣得抱着孩子發抖，忽然見趙七爺滿臉油汗，瞪着眼，準對伊衝過來，便十分害怕，不敢說完話，回身走了。趙七爺也跟着走去，眾人一面怪八一嫂多事，一面讓開路，幾個剪過辮子重新留起的便趕快躲在人叢後面，怕他看見。趙七爺也不細心察訪，通過人叢，忽然轉入烏桕樹後，說道『你能抵擋他麼！』跨上獨木橋，揚長去了。

添	tiān	to have a second helping
沒好氣	méi hǎo qì	in a filthy mood
扎	zhā	to jab at
多嘴	duōzǔi	to speak out of turn
偷漢	tōu hàn	to have an illicit lover
寡婦	guǎfù	widow
撲	pū	sound of something hitting another thing
恰巧	qiàqiǎo	it so happens
磚	zhuān	brick
缺口	qüēkoǔ	a dent, a gaping hole, a gap
檢	jiǎn	to pick up
合上	hé shàng	to fit together
檢查	jiǎnchá	to inspect
一巴掌	yì bāzhǎng	a slap by the palm of the hand
恨棒打人	hèn bàng dǎ rén	most likely a local saying, meaning something like "hitting out in spite"
遶	rào	to go round
大兵	dà bīng	the mighty army
保駕	bǎo jià	to defend the Emperor
張大帥	Zhāng Dà Shuài	Marshal Zhang, i.e., Zhang Xün 張勳
張翼德	Zhāng Yì Dé	Zhang Fei who was one of the brave warriors of the Shu Kingdom
後代	hòudài	descendant
矛	máo	lance
萬夫不當	wàn fū bù dāng	cannot be stopped even by ten thousand men
抵擋	dǐdǎng	to withstand
無形	wúxíng	invisible
搶進	qiǎngjìn	to rush forward ahead of (others or one's opponent)
準	zhǔn	exactly
衝	chōng	to rush against
重新	chóngxīn	to do all over again
人叢	réncóng	crowd
察訪	cháfǎng	to make inquiries, to investigate
跨上	kuà shàng	to step on
揚長去了	yáng cháng ér qù	to stride away with head in air

　　村人們呆呆站着，心裏計算，都覺得自己確乎抵不住張翼德，因此也決定七斤便要沒有性命。七斤既然犯了皇法，想起他往常對人談論城中的新聞的時候，就不該含着長煙管顯出那般驕傲模樣，所以對于七斤的犯法，也覺得有些暢快。他們也彷彿想發些議論，卻又覺得沒有什麼議論可發。嗡嗡的一陣亂嚷，蚊子都撞過赤膊身子，闖到烏柏樹下去做市；他們也就慢慢地走散回家，關上門去睡覺。七斤嫂咕噥着，也收了傢伙和桌子矮凳回家，關上門睡覺了。

　　七斤將破碗拏回家裏，坐在門檻上吸煙；但非常憂愁，忘卻了吸嚥，象牙嘴六尺多長湘妃竹煙管的白銅斗裏的火光，漸漸發黑了。他心裏但覺得事情似乎十分危急，也想想些方法，想些計劃，但總是非常模糊，貫穿不得：『辮子呢辮子？丈八蛇矛。一代不如一代！皇帝坐龍庭。破的碗須得上城去釘好。誰能抵擋他？書上一條一條寫着。入娘的！……』

　　第二日清晨，七斤依舊從魯鎮撐航船進城，傍晚回到魯鎮，又拏着六尺多長的湘妃竹煙管和一個飯碗回村。他在晚飯席上，對九斤老太說，這碗是在城內釘合的，因爲缺口大，所以要十六個銅釘，三文一個，一總用了四十八文小錢。

　　九斤老太很不高興的說，『一代不如一代，我是活夠了。三文錢一個釘；從前的釘，這樣的麼？從前的釘是……我活了七十九歲了，——』

　　此後七斤雖然是照例日日進城，但家景總有些黯

皇法	huángfǎ	the king's law
含着	hán je	with . . . in mouth
驕傲	jiāoào	overbearing
犯法	fàn fǎ	to commit a crime
暢快	chàngkuài	a sense of pleasure
赤膊身子	chì bó shēn zǐ	stripped to the waist
闖	chuǎng	to rush against
做市	zuò shì	to do business
咕噥	gūnóng	to mutter
家(傢)伙	jiāhuǒ	tools, gear
嚥	yàn	to swallow
危急	wēijí	in a critical position
計畫	jìhuà	plan
貫穿	guànchuān	to link up into a unity
席上	xíshàng	at table (for a meal or a meeting)
黯淡	àndàn	gloomy (atmosphere, outlook, etc.)

淡,村人大抵迴避着,不再來聽他從城內得來的新聞。
七斤嫂也沒有好聲氣,還時常叫他『囚徒』。

　　過了十多日,七斤從城內回家,看見他的女人非
常高興,問他說,『你在城裏可聽到些什麼?』

　　『沒有聽到些什麼。』

　　『皇帝坐了龍庭沒有呢?』

　　『他們沒有說。』

　　『咸亨酒店裏也沒有人說麼?』

　　『也沒人說。』

　　『我想皇帝一定是不坐龍庭了。我今天走過趙七
爺的店前,看見他又坐着唸書了,辮子又盤在頂上了,
也沒有穿長衫。』

　　『……』

　　『你想,不坐龍庭了罷?』

　　『我想,不坐了罷。』

　　現在的七斤,是七斤嫂和村人又都早給他相當的
尊敬,相當的待遇了。到夏天,他們仍舊在自家門口
的土場上喫飯;大家見了,都笑嘻嘻的招呼。九斤老
太早已做過八十大壽,仍然不平而且康健。六斤的雙
丫角,已經變成一支大辮子了;伊雖然新近裹脚,卻
還能幫同七斤嫂做事,捧着十八個銅釘的飯碗,在土
場上一瘸一拐的往來。

廻避	huíbì	to avoid (person) (out of dislike or deference)
好聲氣	hǎo shēngqì	a kindly tone of voice [cf. 沒好氣]
相當	xiāngdāng	a certain degree
尊敬	zūnjìng	respect
待遇	dàiyù	treatment
康健	kāngjiàn	healthy (cf. 健康 which tends to be used as a noun)
裹脚	guǒ jiǎo	to bind one's feet
一瘸一拐	yì qüé yì guǎi	limping

故鄉

　　我冒了嚴寒，回到相隔二千餘里，別了二十餘年的故鄉去。

　　時候既然是深冬；漸近故鄉時，天氣又陰晦了，冷風吹進船艙中，嗚嗚的響，從篷隙向外一望，蒼黃的天底下，遠近橫着幾個蕭索的荒村，沒有一些活氣。我的心禁不住悲涼起來了。

　　阿！這不是我二十年來時時記得的故鄉？

　　我所記得的故鄉全不如此。我的故鄉好得多了。但要我記起他的美麗，說出他的佳處來，卻又沒有影像，沒有言辭了。彷彿也就如此。于是我自己解釋說：故鄉本也如此，——雖然沒有進步，也未必有如我所感的悲涼，這只是我自己心情的改變罷了，因為我這次回鄉，本沒有什麼好心緒。

　　我這次是專為了別他而來的。我們多年聚族而居的老屋，已經公同賣給別姓了，交屋的期限，只在本年，所以必須趕在正月初一以前，永別了熟識的老屋，而且遠離了熟識的故鄉，搬家到我在謀食的異地去。

　　第二日清早晨我到了我家的門口了。瓦楞上許多枯草的斷莖當風抖着，正在說明這老屋難免易主的原因。幾房的本家大約已經搬走了，所以很寂靜。我到了自家的房外，我的母親早已迎着出來了，接着便飛

故鄉　Gùxiāng

冒	mào	to brave
嚴寒	yán hán	harsh cold
陰晦	yīnhuì	gloomy, overcast
船艙	chuáncāng	cabin
隙	xì	gap, crack
蒼	cāng	dark blue
蕭索	xiāosuǒ	desolate
荒村	huāng cūn	deserted village
悲涼	beiliáng	forlorn, desolate
時時	shíshí	constantly
佳處	jiāchù	attractive points
影像	yǐngxiàng	image
言辭	yáncí	words
心情	xīnqíng	mood
心緒	xīnxù	mood
專爲	zhuān wèi	specially for
聚族	jùzú	the whole clan together
公同（共同）	gōngtóng (gòng tóng)	jointly
交屋	jiāo wū	handing over of the house
期限	qīxiàn	the final date, the time limit
永別	yǒngbié	to say goodbye forever
熟識	shúshi	familiar
謀食	móu shí	to try to make a living
瓦楞	wǎléng	spaces between tiles
斷莖	duàn jīng	broken stems
抖	dǒu	to tremble
難免	nánmiǎn	bound to, difficult to avoid
易主	yì zhǔ	to change owners, to change hands

出了八歲的姪兒宏兒。

我的母親很高興，但也藏着許多淒涼的神情，敎我坐下，歇息，喝茶，且不談搬家的事。宏兒沒有見過我，遠遠的對面站着只是看。

但我們終于談到搬家的事。我說外間的寓所已經租定了，又買了幾件家具，此外須將家裏所有的木器賣去，再去增添。母親也說好，而且行李也略已齊集，木器不便搬運的，也小半賣去了，只是收不起錢來。

『你休息一兩天，去拜望親戚本家一回，我們便可以走了。』母親說。

『是的。』

『還有閏土，他每到我家來時，總問起你，很想見你一回面。我已經將你到家的大約日期通知他，他也許就要來了。』

這時候，我的腦裏忽然閃出一幅神異的圖畫來：深藍的天空中掛着一輪金黃的圓月，下面是海邊的沙地，都種着一望無際的碧綠的西瓜，其間有一個十一二歲的少年，項帶銀圈，手捏一柄鋼叉，向一匹猹儘力的刺去，那猹卻將身一扭，反從他的胯下逃走了。

這少年便是閏土。我認識他時，也不過十多歲，離現在將有三十年了；那時我的父親還在世，家景也好，我正是一個少爺。那一年，我家是一件大祭祀的值年。這祭祀，說是三十多年纔能輪到一回，所以很鄭重；正月裏供祖像，供品很多，祭器很講究，拜的人也很多，祭器也很要防偷去。我家只有一個忙月（我們

淒涼	qīliáng	desolate
神情	shénqíng	expression (on the face)
歇息	xiēxi	to rest
寓所	yùsuǒ	lodgings
家具	jiājù	furniture
增添	zēngtiān	to add to
略	lüè	more or less
齊集	qíjí	assembled
不便	búbiàn	inconvenient
收不起	shōu bù qǐ	unable to collect
通知	tōngzhī	to notify, to inform
閃	shǎn	to flash
神異	shényì	marvellous, fantastic
種	zhòng	to plant, to grow (plants, etc.)
一望無際	yí wàng wú jì	as far as eye can see
西瓜	xīguā	water melon
項	xiàng	neck
圈	qüān	ring (but not ring worn on finger), necklet
柄	bǐng	handle – measure word for things with handles
猹	zhā	a character invented by Lu Xün for a word in the local dialect: probably a kind of badger
儘（盡）力	jìnlì	with all one's might
刺	cì	to stab at
扭	niǔ	to twist, to wriggle
胯下	kuàxià	between the legs
將有	jiāngyǒu	close on
在世	zàishì	alive
家景	jiājǐng	family circumstances
祭祀	jìsì	sacrifice
值年	zhínían	the year one is on duty
鄭重	zhèngzhòng	solemn
供	gòng	to put on the altar (applies both to the offerings and the images to which the offerings are made)
供品	gòngpǐn	offerings
祭器	jìqì	sacrificial vessels
講究	jiǎngjiu	of choice quality
防	fáng	to guard against

這里給人做工的分三種：整年給一定人家做工的叫長年；按日給人做工的叫短工；自己也種地，只在過年過節以及收租時候來給一定的人家做工的稱忙月），忙不過來，他便對父親說，可以叫他的兒子閏土來管祭器的。

我的父親允許了；我也很高興，因為我早聽到閏土這名字，而且知道他和我彷彿年紀，閏月生的，五行缺土，所以他的父親叫他閏土。他是能裝弶捉小鳥雀的。

我于是日日盼望新年，新年到，閏土也就到了。好容易到了年末，有一日，母親告訴我，閏土來了，我便飛跑的去看。他正在廚房裏，紫色的圓臉，頭戴一頂小氈帽，頸上套一個明晃晃的銀項圈，這可見他的父親十分愛他，怕他死去，所以在神佛面前許下願心，用圈子將他套住了。他見人很怕羞，只是不怕我，沒有旁人的時候，便和我說話，于是不到半日，我們便熟識了。

我們那時候不知道談些什麼，只記得閏土很高興，說是上城之後，見了許多沒有見過的東西。

第二日，我便要他捕鳥。他說：

『這不能。須大雪下了纔好。我們沙地上，下了雪，我掃出一塊空地來，用短棒支起一個大竹匾，撒下粃穀，看鳥雀來喫時，我遠遠地將縛在棒上的繩子只一拉，那鳥雀就罩在竹匾下了。什麼都有：稻雞、角雞、鵓鴣、藍背……』

一定	yídìng	specific
過年過節	guò nián guò jié	during New Year or other festivals
收租	shōu zū	collecting rents
忙不過來	máng bú guò lái	so busy as to be unable to cope
管	guǎn	to take charge of
允許	yǔnxǔ	to agree to (a request)
彷彿	fǎngfú	to be roughly the same
閏月	rùn yüè	intercalary month
五行	wǔ xíng	Five Elements
缺	qüē	to lack
裝	zhuāng	to put together, to fix up, to fit
弶	jiàng	a trap for catching birds or animals with a bow mechanism
盼望	pànwàng	to look forward very much to
年末	nián mò	end of the year
氈帽	zhān mào	felt hat
套	tào	to slip on
明晃晃	mínghuānghuāng	gleaming
許願（心）	xǔ yüàn (xīn)	to make a vow
怕羞	pà xiū	bashful
上城	shàng chéng	to go up to the city
捕	bǔ	to catch
掃	sǎo	to sweep
竹匾	zhú biǎn	large but shallow basket (like a sieve)
撒	sǎ	to scatter
秕穀	bǐgǔ	blighted grain
縛	fú	to bind, to tie
罩	zhào	to trap under a zhao
稻雞	dào jī	water rail
角雞	jiǎo jī	woodcock
鵓鴣	bógū	woodpidgeon

　　我于是又很盼望下雪。

　　閏土又對我說：

　　『現在太冷，你夏天到我們這里來。我們日裏到海邊檢貝殼去，紅的綠的都有，鬼見怕也有，觀音手也有。晚上我和爹管西瓜去，你也去。』

　　『管賊麼？』

　　『不是。走路的人口渴了摘一個瓜喫，我們這里是不算偷的。要管的是獾豬、刺蝟、猹。月亮地下，你聽，啦啦的響了，猹在咬瓜了。你便捏了胡叉，輕輕地走去……』

　　我那時並不知道這所謂猹的是怎麼一件東西——便是現在也沒有知道——只是無端的覺得狀如小狗而很凶猛。

　　『他不咬人麼？』

　　『有胡叉呢。走到了，看見猹了，你便刺。這畜生很伶俐，倒向你奔來，反從胯下竄了。他的皮毛是油一般的滑……』

　　我素不知道天下有這許多新鮮事：海邊有如許五色的貝殼；西瓜有這樣危險的經歷，我先前單知道他在水果店裏出賣罷了。

　　『我們沙地裏，潮汛要來的時候，就有許多跳魚兒只是跳，都有青蛙似的兩個脚……』

　　阿！閏土的心裏有無窮無盡的希奇的事，都是我往常的朋友所不知道的。他們不知道一些事，閏土在海邊時，他們都和我一樣只看見院子裏高牆上的四角

貝殼	bèi ké	shells
管	guǎn	to keep watch over
管賊	guǎn zéi	on the look-out for thieves
摘	zhāi	to pluck
獾豬	huānzhū	badger
刺猬	cìwèi	hedgehog
胡叉	húchā	pitchfork
無端	wúduān	for no reason at all
畜生	chùshēng	animal
伶俐	·línglì	clever
竄	cuàn	to get away
素不	sù bū	never
新鮮	xīnxiān	novel
如許	rúxǔ	such (quantity)
經歷	jīnglì	experiences
潮汛	cháoxùn	spring tide
無窮無盡	wú qiúng wú jìn	inexhaustible
希奇	xīqí	rare and wonderful
往常	wǎngcháng	(habitually) in the past

的天空。

可惜正月過去了，閏土須回家裏去，我急得大哭，他也躲到廚房裏，哭着不肯出門，但終于被他父親帶走了。他後來還託他的父親帶給我一包貝殼和幾支很好看的鳥毛，我也曾送他一兩次東西，但從此沒有再見面。

現在我的母親提起了他，我這兒時的記憶，忽而全都閃電似的蘇生過來，似乎看到了我的美麗的故鄉了。我應聲說：

『這好極！他，——怎樣？……』

『他？……他景況也很不如意……』母親說着，便向房外看，『這些人又來了。說是買木器，順手也就隨便拿走的，我得去看看。』

母親站起身，出去了。門外有幾個女人的聲音，我便招宏兒走近面前，和他閒話：問他可會寫字，可願意出門。

『我們坐火車去麼？』

『我們坐火車去。』

『船呢？』

『先坐船，……』

『哈！這模樣了！鬍子這麼長了！』一種尖利的怪聲突然大叫起來。

我喫了一嚇，趕忙擡起頭，卻見一個凸顴骨，薄嘴唇，五十歲上下的女人站在我面前，兩手搭在髀間，沒有繫裙，張着兩腳，正像一個畫圖儀器裏細脚伶仃

可惜	kěxī	a pity
須	xū	to have to
急	jí	to be in a state
託	tuō	to ask someone to do something on your behalf
提起	tíqǐ	to mention
閃電	shǎndiàn	in a lightning flash
蘇生	sūshēng	to revive
不如意	bù rú yì	for things not to go well
順手	shùnshǒu	to do something else as well while you are at it
出門	chūmén	to travel
這模樣了	zhè móyàng le	he has grown to be such a man
尖利	jiānlì	sharp, hence shrill
喫了一嚇	chī le hí xià	to be given a fright
凸	tū	protruding
顴骨	quángǔ	cheek bones
搭	dā	to rest on
髀	bǐ	thighs
髀間	bǐ jiān	the hips (in this context)
畫圖	huàtú	drawing
儀器	yíqì	instruments
細脚伶仃	xì jiǎo língdīng	with thin legs

的圓規。

　　我愕然了。

　　『不認識了麼？我還抱過你咧！』

　　我愈加愕然了。幸而我的母親也就進來，從旁說：

　　『他多年出門，統忘卻了。你該記得罷，』便向着我說，『這是斜對門的楊二嫂，……開豆腐店的。』

　　哦，我記得了。我孩子時候，在斜對門的豆腐店裏確乎終日坐着一個楊二嫂，人都叫伊『豆腐西施』。但是擦着白粉，顴骨沒有這麼高，嘴唇也沒有這麼薄，而且終日坐着，我也從沒有見過這圓規式的姿勢。那時人說：因爲伊，這豆腐店的買賣非常好。但這大約因爲年齡的關係，我卻並未蒙着一毫感化，所以竟完全忘卻了。然而圓規很不平，顯出鄙夷的神色，彷彿嗤笑法國人不知道拿破崙，美國人不知道華盛頓似的，冷笑說：

　　『忘了？這眞是貴人眼高……』

　　『那有這事……我……』我惶恐着，站起來說。

　　『那麼，我對你說。迅哥兒，你闊了，搬動又笨重，你還要什麼這些破爛木器，讓我拿去罷。我們小戶人家，用得着。』

　　『我並沒有闊哩。我須賣了這些，再去……』

　　『阿呀呀，你放了道臺了，還說不闊？你現在有三房姨太太；出門便是八擡的大轎，還說不闊？嚇，什麼都瞞不過我。』

　　我知道無話可說了，便閉了口，默默的站着。

圓規	yüánguī	pair of compasses
愕然	èrán	taken aback
愈加	yùjiā	even more
統（統）	tǒng (tǒng)	totally
斜對門	xié duìmén	opposite (but not exactly)
開	kāi	to keep (a shop)
西施	Xī Shī	famous beauty of the Spring and Autumn Period
擦	cā	to put on powder; to rub
式	shì	(suff.) style
姿勢	zīshì	posture
買賣	mǎimài	business
年齡	niánlíng	age
…的關係…	… de guānxi	on account of …
蒙	méng	to receive (from superior) (honorific)
感化	gǎnhuà	transforming (reforming) influence
不平	bùpíng	to feel unjustly treated, to have grounds for complaint
鄙夷	bǐyí	contemptuous
嗤笑	chīxiào	to mock at
拿破崙	Ná Pò Lún	Napoleon
華盛頓	Huá Shèng Dùn	Washington
貴人眼高	guìrén yǎn gāo	a man of consequence who would not deign to look at us
惶恐	huángkǒng	in fear and trembling
闊	kuò	affluent, in style
笨重	bènzhòng	heavy and awkward to move
小戶人家	xiǎo hù rén jiā	poor family
用得着	yòng dé zháo	to come in useful
放	fàng	to be appointed to an official post outside the capital
道臺	dàotái	intendant of a circuit
三房姨太太	sānfáng yítàitai	three concubines
八擡的大橋	bā tái de dà jiào	a sedan chair carried by eight carriers only officials of very high rank are entitled to
瞞	mán	to keep something from someone

『阿呀阿呀，真是愈有錢，便愈是一毫不肯放鬆，愈是一毫不肯放鬆，便愈有錢……』圓規一面憤憤的回轉身，一面絮絮的說，慢慢向外走，順便將我母親的一副手套塞在褲腰裏，出去了。

此後又有近處的本家和親戚來訪問我。我一面應酬，偷空便收拾些行李，這樣的過了三四天。

一日是天氣很冷的午後，我喫過午飯，坐着喝茶，覺得外面有人進來了，便回頭去看。我看時，不由的非常出驚，慌忙站起身，迎着走去。

這來的便是閏土。雖然我一見便知道是閏土，但又不是我這記憶上的閏土了。他身材增加了一倍；先前的紫色的圓臉，已經變作灰黃，而且加上了很深的皺紋；眼睛也像他父親一樣，周圍都腫得通紅，這我知道，在海邊種地的人，終日吹着海風，大抵是這樣的。他頭上是一頂破氈帽，身上只一件極薄的棉衣，渾身瑟索着；手裏提着一個紙包和一支長煙管，那手也不是我所記得的紅活圓實的手，卻又粗又笨而且開裂，像是松樹皮了。

我這時很興奮，但不知道怎麼說纔好，只是說：

『阿！閏土哥，——你來了？……』

我接着便有許多話，想要連珠一般湧出：角雞、跳魚兒、貝殼、猹，……但又總覺得被什麼擋着似的，單在腦裏面回旋，吐不出口外去。

他站住了，臉上現出歡喜和凄涼的神情；動着嘴唇，卻沒有作聲。他的態度終于恭敬起來了，分明的

一毫不肯放鬆	yì háo bù kěn fàngsōng	would not let others off with the least advantage
絮絮	xùxù	to go on and on
手套	shǒutào	gloves
褲腰	kùyāo	top of the trousers
應酬	yìngchóu	to cope with visitors, guests, etc.
偷空	tōu kòng	to snatch a moment
收拾	shōushí	to put in order
皺紋	zhòuwén	wrinkles
腫	zhǒng	puffed, swollen
渾身	húnshēn	all over
瑟索（縮）	sèsuō	to tremble
活	huó	supple
圓實	yüánshí	round and firm
連珠	liánzhū	string of pearls
湧出	yǒng chū	to gush out, to well up
回旋	húixüán	to go round and round
吐	tǔ	to spit – to get out of one's mouth
態度	tàidù	attitude
恭敬	gōngjìng	respectful

叫道：

　　『老爺！……』

　　我似乎打了一個寒噤；我就知道，我們之間已經隔了一層可悲的厚障壁了。我也說不出話。

　　他回過頭去說，『水生，給老爺磕頭。』便拖出躲在背後的孩子來，這正是一個廿年前的閏土，只是黃瘦些，頸子上沒有銀圈罷了。『這是第五個孩子，沒有見過世面，躲躲閃閃……』

　　母親和宏兒下樓來了，他們大約也聽到了聲音。

　　『老太太。信是早收到了。我實在喜歡的了不得，知道老爺回來……』閏土說。

　　『阿，你怎的這樣客氣起來。你們先前不是哥弟稱呼麼？還是照舊：迅哥兒。』母親高興的說。

　　『阿呀，老太太真是……這成什麼規矩，那時是孩子，不懂事……』閏土說着，又叫水生上來打拱，那孩子卻害羞，緊緊的只貼在他背後。

　　『他就是水生？第五個？都是生人，怕生也難怪的；還是宏兒和他去走走。』母親說。

　　宏兒聽得這話，便來招水生，水生卻鬆鬆爽爽同他一路出去了。母親叫閏土坐，他遲疑了一回，終於就了坐，將長煙管靠在桌旁，遞過紙包來，說：

　　『冬天沒有什麼東西了。這一點乾青豆倒是自家曬在那里的，請老爺……』

　　我問問他的景況。他只是搖頭。

　　『非常難。第六個孩子也會幫忙了，卻總是喫不

寒噤	hánjìn	shudder
障壁	zhàngbì	a wall
磕頭	kē tóu	to kowtow
見過世面	jiàn guò shì miàn	to have seen the world
躲躲閃閃	duǒduǒ shǎnshǎn	constantly trying to hide, shy
哥弟稱呼	gē dì chēnghū	addressing each other as brothers
規矩	guijǔ	manners
不懂事	bù dǒng shì	did not know any better
打拱	dǎ gǒng	to bow
貼	tiē	to stick — to keep close to
生人	shēngrén	stranger
鬆鬆爽爽	sōngsōng shuǎngshuǎng	free and easy

夠……又不太平……什麼地方都要錢，沒有定規……
收成又壞。種出東西來，挑去賣，總要捐幾回錢，折
了本；不去賣，又只能爛掉……』

　　他只是搖頭；臉上雖然刻着許多皺紋，卻全然不
動，彷彿石像一般。他大約只是覺得苦，卻又形容不
出，沈默了片時，便拿起煙管來默默的吸煙了。

　　母親問他，知道他的家裏事務忙，明天便得回去；
又沒有喫過午飯，便叫他自己到廚下炒飯喫去。

　　他出去了；母親和我都歎息他的景況：多子、饑
荒、苛稅、兵、匪、官、紳，都苦得他像一個木偶人
了。母親對我說，凡是不必搬走的東西，儘可以送他，
可以聽他自己去揀擇。

　　下午，他揀好了幾件東西：兩條長桌，四個椅子，
一副香爐和燭臺，一桿擡秤。他又要所有的草灰（我
們這里煮飯是燒稻草的，那灰，可以做沙地的肥料），
待我們啓程的時候，他用船來載去。

　　夜間，我們又談些閒天，都是無關緊要的話；第
二天早晨，他就領了水生回去了。

　　又過了九日，是我們啓程的日期。閏土早晨便到
了，水生沒有同來，卻只帶着一個五歲的女兒管船隻。
我們終日很忙碌，再沒有談天的工夫。來客也不少，
有送行的，有拿東西的，有送行兼拿東西的。待到傍
晚我們上船的時候，這老屋裏的所有破舊大小粗細東
西，已經一掃而空了。

　　我們的船向前走，兩岸的青山在黃昏中，都裝成

太平	tàipíng	peaceful (absence of war)
定規	dìnggui	fixed rule
收成	shōuchéng	harvest
挑	tiāo	to carry in two baskets with a pole over the shoulder
捐	jüān	to pay a levy
折了本	shé le běn	to have lost money in a business
爛	làn	to rot
石像	shí xiàng	stone statue
事務	shìwù	affairs
炒	chǎo	to roast something in a pan by turning it over constantly
饑荒	jīhuāng	famine
苛稅	kē shuì	harsh taxes
匪	fěi	bandits
官	guān	officials
紳	shēn	local gentry
木偶	mùoǔ	wooden figure, puppet
儘可以	jǐn kě yǐ	as far as is possible
揀擇	jiǎnzé	to choose
擡秤	tái chèng	a large steelyard which needs two to operate
稻草	dàocǎo	straw
肥料	féiliào	fertiliser
啓程	qǐ chéng	to depart, to start on one's journey
忙碌	mánglù	busy
粗細	cūxì	gross or refined
一掃而空	yī sǎo ér kōng	emptied in one sweep

了深黛顏色，連着退向船後梢去。

　　宏兒和我靠着船窗，同看外面模糊的風景，他忽然問道：

　　『大伯！我們什麼時候回來？』

　　『回來？你怎麼還沒有走就想回來了。』

　　『可是，水生約我到他家玩去咧……』他睜着大的黑眼睛，癡癡的想。

　　我和母親也都有些惘然，于是又提起閏土來。母親說，那豆腐西施的楊二嫂，自從我家收拾行李以來，本是每日必到的，前天伊在灰堆裏，掏出十多個碗碟來，議論之後，便定說是閏土埋着的，他可以在運灰的時候，一齊搬回家裏去；楊二嫂發見了這件事，自己很以為功，便拿了那狗氣殺（這是我們這里養雞的器具，木盤上面有着栅欄，內盛食料，雞可以伸進頸子去啄，狗卻不能，只能看着氣死），飛也似的跑了，虧伊裝着這麼高低的小脚，竟跑得這樣快。

　　老屋離我愈遠了；故鄉的山水也都漸漸遠離了我，但我卻並不感到怎樣的留戀。我只覺得我四面有看不見的高牆，將我隔成孤身，使我非常氣悶；那西瓜地上的銀項圈的小英雄的影象，我本來十分清楚，現在卻忽地模糊了，又使我非常的悲哀。

　　母親和宏兒都睡着了。

　　我躺着，聽船底潺潺的水聲，知道我在走我的路。我想：我竟與閏土隔絕到這地步了，但我們的後輩還是一氣，宏兒不是正在想念水生麼。我希望他們不再

黛	dài	deep blue paint for eyebrows
後梢	hòushāo	stern
模糊	móhú	indistinct
癡癡的	chīchī de	to be engrossed in, obsessed by
惘然	wǎngrán	lost (in thought)
虧…	kuī	I don't know how . . .
底	dǐ	sole of shoe
小脚	xiǎo jiǎo	small bound feet
留戀	liúliàn	reluctance to leave a place or thing
孤身	gūshēn	a person all by himself
氣悶	qìmèn	suffocated
潺潺的	chánchán de	descriptive of sound of flowing water
隔絕	géjüé	cut off
後輩	hòubèi	one's junior, the next generation
一氣	yíqì	in communion

像我，又大家隔膜起來……然而我又不願意他們因為要一氣，都如我的辛苦展轉而生活，也不願意他們都如閏土的辛苦痲木而生活，也不願意都如別人的辛苦恣睢而生活。他們應該有新的生活，為我們所未經生活過的。

我想到希望，忽然害怕起來了。閏土要香爐和燭臺的時候，我還暗地裏笑他，以為他總是崇拜偶像，什麼時候都不忘卻。現在我所謂希望，不也是我自己手製的偶像麼？只是他的願望切近，我的願望茫遠罷了。

我在朦朧中，眼前展開一片海邊碧綠的沙地來，上面深藍的天空中掛着一輪金黃的圓月。我想：希望是本無所謂有，無所謂無的。這正如地上的路；其實地上本沒有路，走的人多了，也便成了路。

隔膜	gémò	there being a barrier between
展轉	zhǎnzhuǎn	to drift from place to place
麻木	mámù	numb
恣睢	cìsuì	indulgent (literary)
崇拜偶像	chóngbài oǔxiàng	to worship idols
切近	qièjìn	close by, within easy reach
茫遠	mángyüǎn	distant and uncertain of realisation
無所謂有無所謂無	wú suǒ wèi yǒu wú suǒ wèi wú	it is not the kind of thing one can say either that it exists or does not exist

祝福

　　舊曆的年底畢竟最像年底，村鎮上不必說，就在天空中也顯出將到新年的氣象來。灰白色的沈重的晚雲中間時時發出閃光，接着一聲鈍響，是送竈的爆竹；近處燃放的可就更強烈了，震耳的大音還沒有息，空氣裏已經散滿了幽微的火藥香。我是正在這一夜回到我的故鄉魯鎮的。雖說故鄉，然而已沒有家，所以只得暫寓在魯四老爺的宅子裏。他是我的本家，比我長一輩，應該稱之曰『四叔』，是一個講理學的老監生。他比先前並沒有什麼大改變，單是老了些，但也還未留鬍子，一見面是寒暄，寒暄之後說我『胖了』，說我『胖了』之後即大罵其新黨。但我知道，這並非借題在罵我：因為他所罵的還是康有為。但是，談話是總不投機的了，于是不多久，我便一個人剩在書房裏。

　　第二天我起得很遲，午飯之後，出去看了幾個本家和朋友；第三天也照樣。他們也都沒有什麼大改變，單是老了些；家中卻一律忙，都在準備着『祝福』。這是魯鎮年終的大典，致敬盡禮，迎接福神，拜求來年一年中的好運氣的。殺雞，宰鵝，買豬肉，用心細細的洗，女人的臂膊都在水裏浸得通紅，有的還帶着絞絲銀鐲子。煮熟之後，橫七豎八的插些筷子在這類東西上，可就稱為『福禮』了，五更天陳列起來，並

祝福　　Zhùfú

舊曆	jiù lì	the old calendar, i.e. the lunar calendar
畢竟	bìjìng	after all said and done
氣象	qìxiàng	air, appearance
鈍響	dùn xiǎng	heavy thud
送竈	sòng zào	sending off of the god of the cooking range at the end of the year
爆竹	bàozhú	fire crackers
燃放	ránfàng	to let off (fire crackers)
震耳	zhèn ěr	ear shattering
息	xī	to subside, to die down
幽微	yōuwēi	faint
火藥	huǒyào	gun powder
宅子	zhaízu	residence
理學	lǐxüé	Neo-Confucianism
監生	jiànshēng	a degree which is also obtainable in the Ch'ing Dynasty by financial contribution
寒暄	hánxüān	polite exchanges
新黨	xīn dǎng	new party, revolutionaries
借題	jiètí	to get at one thing while overtly talking about something else
不投機	bù tóujī	not to hit it off
剩	shèng	left behind
一律	yílù	uniformly, without exception
大典	dà diǎn	important ceremony
致敬盡禮	zhǐ jìng jìn lǐ	to offer one's respect and do everything that is required by the rites
福神	fú shén	god of blessing
好運氣	hǎo yùnqì	good luck
宰	zǎi	to slaughter
用心	yòngxīn	with care
細細	xìxǐ	meticulously
臂膊	bìbó	arm
絞絲	jiǎosī	twisted
銀鐲子	yín zhúzi	silver bracelet
橫七豎八	héng qī shù bā	in a haphazard manner
陳列	chénliè	to lay out, to array

且點上香燭,恭請福神們來享用;拜的卻只限于男人,拜完自然仍然是放爆竹。年年如此,家家如此,──「 買得起福禮和爆竹之類的,──今年自然也如此。天色愈陰暗了,下午竟下起雪來,雪花大的有梅花那麼大,滿天飛舞,夾着煙靄和忙碌的氣色,將魯鎮亂成一團糟。我回到四叔的書房裏時,瓦楞上已經雪白,房裏也映得較光明,極分明的顯出壁上掛着的朱拓的大『壽』字,陳摶老祖寫的;一邊的對聯已經脫落,鬆鬆的捲了放在長桌上,一邊的還在,道是『事理通達心氣和平』。我又無聊賴的到窗下的案頭去一翻,只見一堆似乎未必完全的《康熙字典》,一部《近思錄集註》和一部《四書襯》。無論如何,我明天決計要走了。

況且,一想到昨天遇見祥林嫂的事,也就使我不能安住。那是下午,我到鎮的東頭訪過一個朋友,走出來,就在河邊遇見她;而且見她瞪着的眼睛的視線,就知道明明是向我走來的。我這回在魯鎮所見的人們中,改變之大,可以說無過于她的了:五年前的花白的頭髮,即今已經全白,全不像四十上下的人;臉上瘦削不堪,黃中帶黑,而且消盡了先前悲哀的神色,彷彿是木刻似的;只有那眼珠間或一輪,還可以表示她是一個活物。她一手提着竹籃,內中一個破碗,空的;一手拄着一支比她更長的竹竿,下端開了裂:她分明已經純乎是一個乞丐了。

我就站住,豫備她來討錢。

香燭	xiāng zhú	joss sticks and candles
只限于	zhǐ xiàn yǔ	limited to
雪花	xüěhuā	snow flakes
夾着	jiā zhe	interspersed with
煙靄	yānǎi	smoke
忙碌的氣色	mánglù de qìsè	bustling atmosphere
亂成一團糟	luàn chéng yì tuán zāo	thrown into total confusion
映得較光明	yìng de jiào guāngmíng	to show up brighter
搨	tà	to make a rubbing
陳摶	Chén Tuán	a Taoist priest at the beginning of the Sung Dynasty who had a great deal to do with the beginnings of Neo-Confucianism
對聯	dùilián	scrolls in couplet
脫落	tuōluò	to come off
道是	daò shǐ	what it says is
無聊賴	wú liáolài	bored with having nothing to do
近思錄集註	Jìn Sǐ Lù Jí Zhù	Collected commentaries on the Jin Si Lu, an anthology of Neo-Confucian writings edited by Chu Hsi
四書襯	Sǐ Shū Qìn	An exegetical work on the Four Books by Luò Péi of the Chǐng Dynasty
無論如何	wú lùn rú hé	whatever happens
安住	ān zhù	to stay on with equanimity
視線	shǐ xiàn	line of vision
無過于	wú guò yǔ	none more than
瘦削	shòuxuē	gaunt, emaciated
不堪	bùkān	(after adjectives) exceedingly
黃中帶黑	huáng zhōng dài hēi	a suggestion of dark colour underneath the sallowness
消盡	xiāo jìn	completely gone
木刻的	mùkè de	cut (carved) in wood
眼珠一輪	yǎnzhū yì lún	with a roll of the eyeballs
拄	zhǔ	to lean against for support
端	duān	end, tip
裂	liè	a split; to split
純乎	chúnhū	purely
站住	zhàn zhù	to halt one's steps

『您回來了？』她先這樣問。

『是的。』

『這正好。你是識字的，又是出門人，見識得多。我正要問你一件事——』她那沒有精釆的眼睛忽然發光了。

我萬料不到她卻說出這樣的話來，詫異的站着。

『就是——』她走近兩步，放低了聲音，極祕密似的切切的說，『一個人死了之後，究竟有沒有魂靈的？』

我很悚然，一見她的眼釘着我的，背上也就遭了芒刺一般，比在學校裏遇到不及豫防的臨時考，教師又偏是站在身旁的時候，惶急得多了。對于魂靈的有無，我自己是向來毫不介意的；但在此刻，怎樣回答她好呢？我在極短期的躊躕中，想，這里的人照例相信鬼，然而她，卻疑惑了，——或者不如說希望：希望其有，又希望其無……。人何必增添末路的人的苦惱，爲她起見，不如說有罷。

『也許有罷，——我想。』我于是吞吞吐吐的說。

『那麼，也就有地獄了？』

『阿！地獄？』我很喫驚，只得支梧着，『地獄？——論理，就該也有。——然而也未必，……誰來管這等事……。』

『那麼，死掉的一家的人，都能見面的？』

『唉唉，見面不見面呢？……』這時我已知道自己也還是完全一個愚人，什麼躊躕，什麼計畫，都擋

識字的	shí zì de	educated
出門人	chū mén rén	one who has travelled
沒有精彩	méi yǒu jīngcǎi	lacklustre
萬料不到	wàn liào bú dào	could not have guessed in a thousand years
詫異	chàyì	surprised
放低	fàngdī	to lower (voice)
切切的	qièqiè de	in a whisper
魂靈	húnlíng	soul
悚然	sǒngrán	having the creeps
芒刺	mángcì	thorn
豫防	yùfáng	to take precautions against
臨時考	línshí kǎo	a snap examination
偏	piàn	as luck would have it
惶急	huángjí	panicky
毫不介意	háo bú jièyì	not to feel the least concern
躊躇	chóuchú	to hesitate
照例	zhàolì	as a rule, as is the rule
疑惑	yíhuò	to have doubts
增添	zēngtiān	to add to
末路	mòlù	the end of the road
苦惱	kúnǎo	miseries, vexation
爲…起見	wèi . . . qǐ jiàn	for the sake of
吞吞吐吐	tūntūn tǔtǔ	hesitant, haltingly
地獄	dìyù	hell
支梧（吾）	zhīwú	to parry, to evade
論理	lùn lǐ	according to what ought to be the case
管	guǎn	to bother with
擋	dǎng	to stand up to

不住三句問。我即刻膽怯起來了，便想全翻過先前的話來，『那是，……實在，我說不清……。其實，究竟有沒有魂靈，我也說不清。』

我乘她不再緊接的問，邁開步便走，恩恩的逃回四叔的家中，心裏很覺得不安逸。自己想，我這答話怕于她有些危險。她大約因爲在別人的祝福時候，感到自身的寂寞了，然而會不會含有別的什麼意思的呢？——或者是有了什麼豫感了？倘有別的意思，又因此發生別的事，則我的答話委實該負若干的責任……。但隨後也就自笑，覺得偶爾的事，本沒有什麼深意義，而我偏要細細推敲，正無怪教育家要說是生着神經病；而況明明說過『說不清』，已經推翻了答話的全局，即使發生什麼事，于我也毫無關係了。

『說不清』是一句極有用的話。不更事的勇敢的少年，往往敢于給人解決疑問，選定醫生，萬一結果不佳，大抵反成了怨府，然而一用這說不清來作結束，便事事逍遙自在了。我在這時，更感到這一句話的必要，即使和討飯的女人說話，也是萬不可省的。

但是我總覺得不安，過了一夜，也仍然時時記憶起來，彷彿懷着什麼不祥的豫感；在陰沈的雪天裏，在無聊的書房裏，這不安愈加強烈了。不如走罷，明天進城去。福興樓的清燉魚翅，一元一大盤，價廉物美，現在不知增價了否？往日同游的朋友，雖然已經雲散，然而魚翅是不可不喫的，即使只有我一個……。無論如何，我明天決計要走了。

膽怯	dǎnqiè	to lose courage, cowardly
翻過	fān guò	to reverse
說不清	shuō bù qīng	too complicated for me to explain
乘	chéng	to take advantage of (opportunity)
再緊接的問	zài jǐnjiē de wèn	to follow up immediately with another question
邁步	mài bù	to step out, to stride
愡愡的	cōngcōng de	hurriedly
不安逸	bù ānyì	ill at ease
豫感	yù gǎn	premonition
委實	wěishí	truly, honestly
負責任	fù zérèn	to bear responsibility
若干	ruògān	a certain amount or number
隨後	suíhòu	afterwards
偶爾	oǔěr	by chance; occasionally
推敲	tuīqiāo	examine (the meaning) minutely
正無怪	zhèng wú guài	no wonder, you cannot blame people for thinking
教育家	jiàoyù jiā	educationalist
神經病	shénjīng bìng	something wrong in the head
全局	quán jú	the whole game – in its entirety
不更事	bù gēng shì	to lack the advantage of experience
勇敢	yǒnggǎn	brave
往往	wǎngwǎng	very often
解決疑問	jiějué yíwèn	to solve problems
選定	xuǎn dìng	to decide on the choice
萬一	wànyī	on the one in ten thousand chance
結果	jiéguǒ	the result
大抵	dàdǐ	generally speaking
怨府	yüànfǔ	target of blame (class.)
結束	jiéshù	to conclude
逍（消）遙自在	xiāoyáo zìzài	carefree, unencumbered with worries
省	shěng	to do without, to cut out, to cut down
清燉	qīng dùn	to steam without added ingredients
魚翅	yúchì	shark's fins
價廉物美	jià lián wù měi	high quality at low price
否	fǒu	classical negative interrogative particle used at end of sentence or in phrase 是否 shì fǒu (is it or is it not?)
雲散	yǘn sàn	scattered like the clouds

　　我因爲常見些但願不如所料，以爲未必竟如所料
的事，卻每每恰如所料的起來，所以很恐怕這事也一
律。果然，特別的情形開始了。傍晚，我竟聽到有些
人聚在內室裏談話，彷彿議論什麼事似的，但不一會，
說話聲也就止了，只有四叔且走而且高聲的說，

　　『不早不遲，偏偏要在這時候，——這就可見是
一個謬種！』

　　我先是詫異，接着是很不安，似乎這話于我有關
係。試望門外，誰也沒有。好容易待到晚飯前他們的
短工來沖茶，我纔得了打聽消息的機會。

　　『剛纔，四老爺和誰生氣呢？』我問。

　　『還不是和祥林嫂？』那短工簡捷的說。

　　『祥林嫂？怎麼了？』我又趕緊的問。

　　『老了。』

　　『死了？』我的心突然緊縮，幾乎跳起來，臉上
大約也變了色。但他始終沒有擡頭，所以全不覺。我
也就鎮定了自己，接着問——

　　『什麼時候死的？』

　　『什麼時候？——昨天夜裏，或者就是今天罷。——
我說不清。』

　　『怎麼死的？』

　　『怎麼死的？——還不是窮死的？』他澹然的回
答，仍然沒有擡頭向我看，出去了。

　　然而我的驚惶卻不過暫時的事，隨着就覺得要來
的事，已經過去，並不必仰仗我自己的『說不清』和

但願	dàn yüàn	only wish
不如	bù rú	not as
所料	suǒ liào	what is conjectured
每每	měiměi	often
恰如	qiàrú	just as
謬種	miù zhǒng	(abusive) preposterous stock
和誰生氣	hé shuí shēng qì	who was he getting angry with?
緊縮	jǐn suō	to contract severely
澹然	dànrán	placidly
仰仗	yǎngzhàng	rely on the help of (something or someone more powerful than oneself)

他之所謂『窮死的』的寬慰，心地已經漸漸輕鬆；不過偶然之間，還似乎有些負疚。晚飯擺出來了，四叔儼然的陪着。我也還想打聽些關于祥林嫂的消息，但知道他雖然讀過『鬼神者二氣之良能也』，而忌諱仍然極多，當臨近祝福時候，是萬不可提起死亡疾病之類的話的；倘不得已，就該用一種替代的隱語，可惜我又不知道，因此屢次想問，而終于中止了。我從他儼然的臉色上，又忽而疑他正以爲我不早不遲，偏要在這時候來打擾他，也是一個謬種，便立刻告訴他明天要離開魯鎮，進城去，趁早放寬了他的心。他也不很留。這樣悶悶的喫完了一餐飯。

冬季日短，又是雪天，夜色早已籠罩了全市鎮。人們都在燈下恩忙，但窗外很寂靜。雪花落在積得厚厚的雪褥上面，聽去似乎瑟瑟有聲，使人更加感得沈寂。我獨坐在發出黃光的菜油燈下，想，這百無聊賴的祥林嫂，被人們棄在塵芥堆中的，看得厭倦了的陳舊的玩物，先前還將形骸露在塵芥裏，從活得有趣的人們看來，恐怕要怪訝她何以還要存在，現在總算被無常打掃得乾乾淨淨了。魂靈的有無，我不知道；然而在現世，則無聊生者不生，即使厭見者不見，爲人爲己，也還都不錯。我靜聽着窗外似乎瑟瑟作響的雪花聲，一面想，反而漸漸的舒暢起來。

然而先前所見所聞的她的半生事迹的斷片，至此也聯成一片了。

她不是魯鎮人。有一年的冬初，四叔家裏要換女

寬慰	kuānwèi	consolation
輕鬆	qīngsōng	light, relaxed, relieved
負疚	fù jiù	sense of guilt
儼然	yǎnrán	with decorum
忌諱	jìhuì	taboos
不得已	bù dé yǐ	there is no alternative
隱語	yǐnyǔ	veiled reference, euphemism
放寬	fàngkuān	to relieve anxiety
悶悶	mènmèn	in suffocating silence
籠罩	lǒngzhào	to cup over, to envelope
褥	rù	under blanket, mattress
百無聊賴	bǎi wú liáolài	with absolutely nothing to occupy one
塵芥	chénjiè	dust heap
厭倦	yànjüàn	to be tired of
陳舊	chénjiù	well-worn
玩物	wánwù	toy
形骸	xínghái	carcass
怪訝	guàiyà	to be surprised, to blame
無常	wúcháng	transience – hence official of underworld who comes for people whose time is up; a term used to translate the Sauskrit word *antiya*
無聊生	wú liáo shēng	with nothing to live for
厭見	yàn jiàn	to be sick of the sight of
爲人爲己	wèi rén wèi jǐ	whether for the sake of others or for one's own sake
不錯	bú cuò	not bad
舒暢	shūchàng	to feel good
事迹	shìjì	events in a man's history
斷片	duàn piàn	fragments
聯成	lián chéng	to piece together
女工	nǚ gōng	maid-servant

工，做中人的衛老婆子帶她進來了，頭上紮着白頭繩，烏裙，藍夾襖，月白背心，年紀大約二十六七，臉色青黃，但兩頰卻還是紅的。衛老婆子叫她祥林嫂，說是自己母家的鄰舍，死了當家人，所以出來做工了。四叔皺了皺眉，四嬸已經知道了他的意思，是在討厭她是一個寡婦。但看她模樣還周正，手腳都壯大，又只是順着眼，不開一句口，很像一個安分耐勞的人，便不管四叔的皺眉，將她留下了。試工期內，她整天的做，似乎閒着就無聊，又有力，簡直抵得過一個男子，所以第三天就定局，每月工錢五百文。

大家都叫她祥林嫂；沒問她姓什麼，但中人是衛家山人，既說是鄰居，那大概也就姓衛了。她不很愛說話，別人問了纔回答，答的也不多。直到十幾天之後，這纔陸續的知道她家裏還有嚴厲的婆婆；一個小叔子，十多歲，能打柴了；她是春天沒了丈夫的；他本來也打柴為生，比她小十歲：大家所知道的就只是這一點。

日子很快的過去了，她的做工卻毫沒有懈，食物不論，力氣是不惜的。人們都說魯四老爺家裏僱着了女工，實在比勤快的男人還勤快。到年底，掃塵，洗地，殺雞，宰鵝，徹夜的煮福禮，全是一人擔當，竟沒有添短工。然而她反滿足，口角邊漸漸的有了笑影，臉上也白胖了。

新年纔過，她從河邊淘米回來時，忽而失了色，說剛纔遠遠地看見一個男人在對岸徘徊，很像夫家的

中人	zhōngrén	middle man, broker
紮	zhá	to tie
夾襖	jiá ǎo	lined jacket
月白	yuèbái	pale blue
頰	jiá	cheek
當家人	dāngjiā rén	husband
皺眉	zhòu méi	to frown
討厭	tǎoyàn	to dislike
模樣	móyàng	looks
周正	zhōuzhèng	well-proportioned
壯大	zhuàngdà	big and strong
順着眼	shùn zhe yǎn	to look where the eyes are naturally turned, i.e. to look on the ground in a docile manner
安分	ān fèn	knowing one's place, content with one's lot and so unlikely to cause trouble
耐勞	nàiláo	able to stand up to hard labour
試工期	shìgōng qī	probationary period
簡直	jiǎnzhí	to all intents and purposes
抵得過	dǐ dé guò	to be as good as
定局	dìngjü	the matter was settled
陸續	lùxü	bit by bit
嚴厲	yánlì	strict, harsh
婆婆	pópó	mother-in-law
小叔子	xiǎoshūzǐ	younger brother of husband
打柴	dǎ chái	to cut firewood
沒了	méi le	lost
懈	xiè	to slacken
食物不論	shí wù bú lùn	not particular about food
不惜力氣	bù xī lìqì	to spare no effort
僱	gù	to hire
勤快	qínkuài	industrious and quick
徹夜	chèyè	all through the night
擔當	dāndāng	to take on, to shoulder
淘米	táo mǐ	to wash rice
失了色	shī le sè	drenched of colour

堂伯，恐怕是正爲尋她而來的。四嬸很驚疑，打聽底
細，她又不說。四叔一知道，就皺一皺眉，道：

『這不好。恐怕她是逃出來的。』

她誠然是逃出來的，不多久，這推想就證實了。

此後大約十幾天，大家正已漸漸忘卻了先前的事，
衞老婆子忽而帶了一個三十多歲的女人進來了，說那
是祥林嫂的婆婆。那女人雖是山裏人模樣，然而應酬
很從容，說話也能幹，寒暄之後，就賠罪，說她特來
叫她的兒媳回家去，因爲開春事務忙，而家中只有老
的和小的，人手不夠了。

『旣是她的婆婆要她回去，那有什麼話可說呢。』
四叔說。

于是算清了工錢，一共一千七百五十文，她全存
在主人家，一文也還沒有用，便都交給她的婆婆。那
女人又取了衣服，道過謝，出去了。其時已經是正午。

『阿呀，米呢？祥林嫂不是去淘米的麼？……』
好一會，四嬸這纔驚叫起來。她大約有些餓，記得午
飯了。

于是大家分頭尋淘籮。她先到廚下，次到堂前，
後到臥房，全不見淘籮的影子。四叔踱出門外，也不
見，直到河邊，纔見平平正正的放在岸上，旁邊還有
一株菜。

看見的人報告說，河裏面上午就泊了一隻白篷船，
篷是全蓋起來的，不知道什麼人在裏面，但事前也沒
有人去理會他。待到祥林嫂出來淘米，剛剛要跪下去，

恐怕	kǒngpà	I am afraid (something is the case)
打聽底細	dǎ ting dǐxì	to find out the details
誠然	chéngrán	(lit.) truly
推想	tuīxiǎng	inference
證實	zhèngshí	proved to be the case
從容	cōngróng	unhurried, self-possessed
能幹	nénggàn	able
賠罪	péi zuì	to apologise
特	tè	specially
兒媳	érxí	daughter-in-law
開春	kāichūn	with the coming of the new year
事務	shìwù	affairs
人手	rénshǒu	hands
算清	suàn qīng	to make a final reckoning
存在	cún zài	deposited with
道謝	dào xiè	to say thank you
分頭	fēntou	in different directions
籮	luó	basket
平平正正	píngpíng zhèngzhèng	squarely
株	zhū	measure word for vegetables, plants, trees
報告	bàogào	to report
泊	bó	to moor
理會	lǐhuì	to pay attention to

那船裏便突然跳出兩個男人來，像是山裏人，一個抱住她，一個幫着，拖進船去了。祥林嫂還哭喊了幾聲，此後便再沒有什麼聲息，大約給用什麼堵住了罷。接着就走上兩個女人來，一個不認識，一個就是衞婆子。窺探艙裏，不很分明，她像是綑了躺在船板上。

『可惡！然而……。』四叔說。

這一天是四嬸自己煮午飯；他們的兒子阿牛燒火。

午飯之後，衞老婆子又來了。

『可惡！』四叔說。

『你是什麼意思？虧你還會再來見我們。』四嬸洗着碗，一見面就憤憤的說，『你自己薦她來，又合夥劫她去，鬧得沸反盈天的，大家看了成個什麼樣子？你拿我們家裏開玩笑麼？』

『阿呀阿呀，我真上當。我這回，就是為此特地來說說清楚的。她來求我薦地方，我那里料得到是瞞着她的婆婆的呢。對不起，四老爺，四太太。總是我老發昏不小心，對不起主顧。幸而府上是向來寬洪大量，不肯和小人計較的。這回我一定薦一個好的來折罪……。』

『然而……。』四叔說。

于是祥林嫂事件便告終結，不久也就忘卻了。

只有四嬸，因為後來僱用的女工，大抵非懶即饞，或者饞而且懶，左右不如意，所以也還提起祥林嫂。每當這些時候，她往往自言自語的說，『她現在不知道怎麼樣了？』意思是希望她再來。但到第二年的新

聲息	shēngxī	sound and breathing, hence sign of presence of human being
堵	dǔ	to block up, to gag
窺探	kuītàn	to peep into, to spy
綑	kǔn	to bind, to tie up
船板	chuánbǎn	deck
可惡	kěwù	disgraceful
薦	jiàn	to recommend
合夥	héhuǒ	to be in it with; to be in partnership with
劫	jié	to kidnap
沸反盈天	fèi fǎn yíng tiān	to create a commotion
上當	shàng dàng	to be taken in, to be led up the garden path
瞞着	mán zhē	behind someone's back
老發昏	lǎo fā hūn	muddle-headed in my senility
對不起	duì bù qǐ	[takes direct object] I am sorry, it was all due to, put it all down to
主顧	zhǔgù	customer
寬洪大量	kuān hóng dà liàng	magnanimous
計較	jìjiào	to hold it against
這回	zhè huí	this time [n.b. in this context, next time]
折罪	zhézuì	to make up for it
告終結	gào zhōngjié	came to a close
非x 即y	fēi x jí y	either x or y
x 而且y	x ér qiě y	both x and y
不如意	bù rúyì	not satisfactory to, not as one would have liked
提起	tíqǐ	to mention
新正	xīnzhēng	the first month of the new year

正，她也就絕了望。

新正將盡，衞老婆子來拜年了，已經喝得醉醺醺的，自說因爲回了一趟衞家山的娘家，住下幾天，所以來得遲了。她們問答之間，自然就談到祥林嫂。

『她麼？』衞老婆子高興的說，『現在是交了好運了。她婆婆來抓她回去的時候，是早已許給了賀家墺的賀老六的，所以回家之後不幾天，也就裝在花轎裏擡去了。』

『阿呀，這樣的婆婆！……』四嬸驚奇的說。

『阿呀，我的太太！你眞是大戶人家的太太的話。我們山裏人，小戶人家，這算得什麼？她有小叔子，也得娶老婆。不嫁了她，那有這一注錢來做聘禮？她的婆婆倒是精明強幹的女人呵，很有打算，所以就將她嫁到裏山去。倘許給本村人，財禮就不多；惟獨肯嫁進深山野墺裏去的女人少，所以她就到手了八十千。現在第二個兒子的媳婦也娶進了，財禮只花了五十，除去辦喜事的費用，還剩十多千。嚇，你看，這多麼好打算？……』

『祥林嫂竟肯依？……』

『這有什麼依不依。──鬧是誰也總要鬧一鬧的；只要用繩子一綑，塞在花轎裏，擡到男家，捺上花冠，拜堂，關上房門，就完事了。可是祥林嫂眞出格，聽說那時實在鬧得利害，大家還都說大約因爲在唸書人家做過事，所以與衆不同呢。太太，我們見得多了：回頭人出嫁，哭喊的也有，說要尋死覓活的也有，擡

醉醺醺	zuìxūnxūn	tipsy
娘家	niángjiā	wife's own family
交	jiāo	to have entered a period of (good or bad) luck
花轎	huājiào	bridal sedan chair
一注	yí zhù	a sum (of money)
聘禮	pìnglǐ	betrothal gift
精明	jīngmíng	sharp-witted, astute
有打算	yǒu dǎsuàn	shrewd, (able to reckon which course of action is the most advantageous)
墺	aò	remote mountain region
辦喜事	bàn xǐshì	to organise celebrations
費用	fèiyòng	expenses
依	yī	to do as one is told
鬧	nào	to kick up a fuss
只要	zhǐyào	all you have to do is
捺	nà	to press down on
花冠	huāguān	bridal headgear
拜堂	bài táng	ceremony to solemnise the wedding
出格	chūgé	exceptional, distinguished
與衆不同	yǔ zhòng bù tóng	quite different from the run of the mill
尋死覓活	xún sǐ mǐ huó	to threaten to kill oneself

到男家鬧得拜不成天地的也有，連花燭都砸了的也有。祥林嫂可是異乎尋常，他們說她一路只是嚎，罵，擡到賀家墺，喉嚨已經全啞了。拉出轎來，兩個男人和她的小叔子使勁的擒住她也還拜不成天地。他們一不小心，一鬆手，阿呀，阿彌陀佛，她就一頭撞在香案角上，頭上碰了一個大窟窿，鮮血直流，用了兩把香灰，包上兩塊紅布還止不住血呢。直到七手八脚的將她和男人反關在新房裏，還是罵，阿呀呀，這眞是……。』她搖一搖頭，順下眼睛，不說了。

　　『後來怎麼樣呢？』四嬸還問。

　　『聽說第二天也沒有起來。』她擡起眼來說。

　　『後來呢？』

　　『後來？——起來了。她到年底就生了一個孩子，男的，新年就兩歲了。我在娘家這幾天，就有人到賀家墺去，回來說看見他們娘兒倆，母親也胖，兒子也胖；上頭又沒有婆婆；男人所有的是力氣，會做活；房子是自家的。——唉唉，她眞是交了好運了。』

　　從此之後，四嬸也就不再提起祥林嫂。

　　但有一年的秋季，大約是得到祥林嫂好運的消息之後的又過了兩個新年，她竟又站在四叔家的堂前了。桌上放着一個荸薺式的圓籃；簷下一個小鋪蓋。她仍然頭上紮着白頭繩，烏裙，藍夾襖，月白背心，臉色青黃，只是兩頰上已經消失了血色，順着眼，眼角上帶些淚痕，眼光也沒有先前那樣精神了。而且仍然是衞老婆子領着，顯出慈悲模樣，絮絮的對四嬸說，

砸	zá	to break
異乎	yìhū	(lit.) different from
尋常	xúncháng	the ordinary
嚎	háo	to howl
啞	yǎ	dumb, hoarse
使勁	shǐ jìn	forcefully
擒	cín	to catch hold of
阿彌陀佛	Ē Mí Tuó Fó	Amida Buddha
撞	zhuàng	to knock, to charge at
香案	xiāng'àn	the altar (lit. incense table)
窟窿	kūlōng	a gaping hole
香灰	xiāng huī	incense ash
反關	fǎn guān	locked on the outside
自家的	zìjiā de	one's own
荸薺	bíqí	water chestnut
簷	yán	eaves
鋪蓋	pūgài	bedding
慈悲	cíbēi	merciful; mercy

　　『……這實在是叫作「天有不測風雲」，她的男人是堅實人，誰知道年紀青青，就會斷送在傷寒上？本來已經好了的，喫了一碗冷飯，復發了。幸虧有兒子；她又能做，打柴摘茶養蠶都來得，本來還可以守着，誰知道那孩子又會給狼啣去的呢？春天快完了，村上倒反來了狼，誰料到？現在她只剩了一個光身了。大伯來收屋，又趕她。她真是走投無路了，只好來求老主人。好在她現在已經再沒有什麼牽掛，太太家裏又湊巧要換人，所以我就領她來。——我想，熟門熟路，比生手實在好得多……。』

　　『我真傻，真的，』祥林嫂擡起她沒有神采的眼睛來，接着說。『我單知道下雪的時候野獸在山墺裏沒有食喫，會到村裏來；我不知道春天也會有。我一清早起來就開了門，拿小籃盛了一籃豆，叫我們的阿毛坐在門檻上剝豆去。他是很聽話的，我的話句句聽；他出去了。我就在屋後劈柴，淘米，米下了鍋，要蒸豆。我叫阿毛，沒有應，出去一看，只見豆撒得一地，沒有我們的阿毛了。他是不到別家去玩的；各處去一問，果然沒有。我急了，央人出去尋。直到下半天，尋來尋去尋到山墺裏，看見刺柴上掛着一隻他的小鞋。大家都說，糟了，怕是遭了狼了。再進去；他果然躺在草窠裏，肚裏的五臟已經都給喫空了，手上還緊緊的捏着那隻小籃呢。……』她接着但是嗚咽，說不出成句的話來。

　　四嬸起初還躊躕，待到聽完她自己的話，眼圈就

天有不測風雲	tiān yǒu búcè fēngyún	As there are unpredictable storms
人有旦夕禍福	rén yǒu dànxi huòfú	and clouds in the sky so are there un-predictable ill fortune for man
堅實	jiānshí	solid in build, strapping
青青	qīngqīng	the duplication emphasises the youth-fulness
斷送	duànsòng	to cut short the life of
傷寒	shānghán	typhoid
復發	fù fā	to have a relapse
能做	néng zuò	capable of hard work
守着	shǒu zhe	to maintain her position without deterioration as before
唧（銜）去	xián qù	to carry off (in the mouth)
光身	guāng shēn	all alone in the world
大伯	dàbó	uncle's elder brother
趕	gǎn	to chase out
走投無路	zǒu tóu wú lù	nowhere to turn to
老	lǎo	old — former
牽掛	qiānguà	ties
湊巧	còuqiǎo	it so happened
我想	wǒ xiǎng	it occurred to me
熟門熟路	shú mén shú lù	knowing the ropes
生手	shēngshǒu	new hand
傻	shǎ	stupid
沒有神采	méi yǒu shéncǎi	lacklustre (cf. 沒有精采)
剝	bō	to remove the skin or shell
聽話	tīng huà	obedient
劈柴	pī chái	to chop up wood
撒	sǎ	to scatter
央	yāng	to beg (someone to do something)
刺柴	cìchái	bramble
糟了	zāo le	oh! dear!
草窠	cǎowō	lair
五臟	wǔ zàng	entrails
嗚咽	wūyè	to sob
成句	chéng jù	whole sentence
眼圈	yǎnquān	the rims of the eyes

有些紅了。她想了一想，便教拿圓籃和鋪蓋到下房去。
衞老婆子彷彿卸了一肩重擔似的噓一口氣；祥林嫂比
初來時候神氣舒暢些，不待指引，自己馴熟的安放了
鋪蓋。她從此又在魯鎮做女工了。

　　大家仍然叫她祥林嫂。

　　然而這一回，她的境遇卻改變得非常大。上工之
後的兩三天，主人們就覺得她手腳已沒有先前一樣靈
活，記性也壞得多，死屍似的臉上又整日沒有笑影，
四嬸的口氣上，已頗有些不滿了。當她初到的時候，
四叔雖然照例皺過眉，但鑑于向來僱用女工之難，也
就並不大反對，只是暗暗地告誡四嬸說，這種人雖然
似乎很可憐，但是敗壞風俗的，用她幫忙還可以，祭
祀時候可用不着她沾手，一切飯菜，只好自己做，否
則，不乾不淨，祖宗是不喫的。

　　四叔家裏最重大的事件是祭祀，祥林嫂先前最忙
的時候也就是祭祀，這回她卻清閒了。桌子放在堂中
央，繫上桌幃，她還記得照舊的去分配酒盃和筷子。

　　『祥林嫂，你放着罷！我來擺。』四嬸慌忙的說。

　　她訕訕的縮了手，又去取燭臺。

　　『祥林嫂，你放着罷！我來拿。』四嬸又慌忙的
說。

　　她轉了幾個圓圈，終于沒有事情做，只得疑惑的
走開。她在這一天可做的事是不過坐在竈下燒火。

　　鎮上的人們也仍然叫她祥林嫂，但音調和先前很
不同；也還和她講話，但笑容卻冷冷的了。她全不理

下房	xiàfáng	servants quarters
卸	xiè	to lower burden (from one's shoulders)
嘘一口氣	xū yì kǒu qì	to heave a sigh of relief
神氣舒暢	shénqì shūchàng	to be at ease
指引	zhǐyǐn	to be shown the way
馴〔mistake for 純〕熟	chúnshú	in a practised manner
安放	ānfàng	to put a thing down properly, in its proper place
境遇	jìngyù	circumstances
上工	shàng gōng	to start a job
靈活	línghuó	agile
照例	zhào lì	true to form
鑒于	jiànyú	in view of (referring to lesson learned)
告誡	gàojiè	to warn against
敗壞風俗	bàihuài fēngsú	to have a bad influence on the customs (morals) of the place
沾手	zhān shǒu	to come into the least contact
否則	fǒuzé	otherwise
清閒	qīngxián	(of job) with little to do
繫	xì	to tie
桌幃	zhuōwéi	a square piece of cloth hanging down the front of a table
分配	fēnpèi	to distribute
酒盃（杯）	jiǔ bēi	wine cup
放着	fàng zhe	to leave a thing as it is, to leave it alone
擺	bǎi	to set out, to lay out
訕訕	shànshàn	in an embarrassed manner
疑惑	yíhuò	not knowing what was wrong
音調	yīndiào	tone

會那些事，只是直着眼睛，和大家講她自己日夜不忘
的故事——

　　『我真傻，真的，』她說。『我單知道雪天是野
獸在深山裏沒有食喫，會到村裏來；我不知道春天也
會有。我一大早起來就開了門，拿小籃盛了一籃豆，
叫我們的阿毛坐在門檻上剝豆去。他是很聽話的孩子，
我的話句句聽；他就出去了。我就在屋後劈柴，淘米，
米下了鍋，打算蒸豆。我叫，「阿毛！」沒有應。出
去一看，只見豆撒得滿地，沒有我們的阿毛了。各處
去一問，都沒有。我急了，央人去尋去。直到下半天，
幾個人尋到山墺裏，看見刺柴上掛着一隻他的小鞋。
大家都說，完了，怕是遭了狼了。再進去；果然，他
躺在草窠裏，肚裏的五臟已經都給喫空了，可憐他手
裏還緊緊的捏着那隻小籃呢。……』她于是淌下眼淚
來，聲音也嗚咽了。

　　這故事倒頗有效，男人聽到這里，往往斂起笑容，
沒趣的走了開去；女人們卻不獨寬恕了她似的，臉上
立刻改換了鄙薄的神氣，還要陪出許多眼淚來。有些
老女人沒有在街頭聽到她的話，便特意尋來，要聽她
這一段悲慘的故事。直到她說到嗚咽，她們也就一齊
流下那停在眼角上的眼淚，歎息一番，滿足的去了，
一面還紛紛的評論着。

　　她就只是反覆的向人說她悲慘的故事，常常引住
了三五個人來聽她。但不久，大家也都聽得純熟了，
便是最慈悲的唸佛的老太太們，眼裏也再不見有一點

淌下	tǎng xià	to let fall (tears)
頗	pō	considerably (class.)
有效	yǒu xiào	effective
斂起	liàn qǐ	to gather up
沒趣的	méiqù de	disconcerted
寬恕	kuānshù	to forgive
鄙薄	bǐbó	comtemptuous
陪出	péi chū	to be out of pocket (in a transaction)
一番	yì fān	a round of (an activity)
紛紛的	fēnfēn de	everyone doing it at the same time
評論	pínglùn	to comment
反覆	fǎnfù	over and over again
引住	yǐn zhù	holding the attention
純熟	chúnshú	familiar, to know well
唸佛	niàn fó	to repeat the name of the Buddha, to worship the Buddha

淚的痕迹。後來全鎭的人們幾乎都能背誦她的話，一聽到就煩厭得頭痛。

　　『我眞傻，眞的，』她開首說。

　　『是的，你是單知道雪天野獸在深山裏沒有食喫，纔會到村裏來的。』他們立即打斷她的話，走開去了。

　　她張着口怔怔的站着，直着眼睛看他們，接着也就走了，似乎自己也覺得沒趣。但她還妄想，希圖從別的事，如小籃，豆，別人的孩子上，引出她的阿毛的故事來。倘一看見兩三歲的小孩子，她就說：

　　『唉唉，我們的阿毛如果還在，也就有這麼大了。……』

　　孩子看見她的眼光就喫驚，牽着母親的衣襟催她走。于是又只剩下她一個，終于沒趣的也走了。後來大家又都知道了她的脾氣，只要有孩子在眼前，便似笑非笑的先問她，道：

　　『祥林嫂，你們的阿毛如果還在，不是也就有這麼大了麼？』

　　她未必知道她的悲哀經大家咀嚼賞鑑了許多天，早已成爲渣滓，只值得煩厭和唾棄；但從人們的笑影上，也彷彿覺得這又冷又尖，自己再沒有開口的必要了。她單是一瞥他們，並不回答一句話。

　　魯鎭永遠是過新年，臘月二十以後就忙起來了。四叔家裏這回須僱男短工，還是忙不過來，另叫柳媽做幫手。殺雞，宰鵝；然而柳媽是善女人，喫素，不殺生的，只肯洗器皿。祥林嫂除燒火之外，沒有別的

背誦	bèisòng	to repeat from memory
開首	kāishǒu	to begin
打斷	dǎ duàn	to interrupt
妄想	wàngxiǎng	to hope for something out of reach
希圖	xītú	hoping to achieve
引出	yǐn chū	to lead on to
衣襟	yījīn	the lapels
催	cuī	to hurry (someone)
咀嚼	jǔjüé	to chew over
賞鑑	shǎngjiàn	to admire, to appreciate (e.g. work of art)
渣滓	zhāzǐ	dregs
唾棄	tuòqì	to despise, discard
一瞥	yì piē	a sidelong glance
臘月	làyüè	the last month of the lunar year
善女人	shàn nürén	a believer (woman) in the Buddha
喫素	chī sù	to be a vegetarian
不殺生	bù shā shēng	to refrain from killing living creatures (Buddhist)
器皿	qìmǐng	utensils

事，卻閒着了，坐着只看柳媽洗器皿。微雪點點的下來了。

『唉唉，我眞傻，』祥林嫂看了天空，歎息着，獨語似的說。

『祥林嫂，你又來了。』柳媽不耐煩的看着她的臉，說。『我問你：你額角上的傷疤，不就是那時撞壞的麼？』

『唔唔。』她含胡的回答。

『我問你：你那時怎麼後來竟依了呢？』

『我麼？……』

『你呀。我想：這總是你自己願意了，不然……。』

『阿阿，你不知道他力氣多麼大呀。』

『我不信。我不信你這麼大的力氣，眞會拗他不過。你後來一定是自己肯了，倒推說他力氣大。』

『阿阿，你……你倒自己試試看。』她笑了。

柳媽的打皺的臉也笑起來，使她蹙縮得像一個核桃；乾枯的小眼睛一看祥林嫂的額角，又釘住她的眼。祥林嫂似乎很局促了，立刻斂了笑容，旋轉眼光，自去看雪花。

『祥林嫂，你實在不合算。』柳媽詭祕的說。『再一强，或者索性撞一個死，就好了。現在呢，你和你的第二個男人過活不到兩年，倒落了一件大罪名。你想，你將來到陰司去，那兩個死鬼的男人還要爭，你給了誰好呢？閻羅大王只好把你鋸開來，分給他們。我想，這眞是……。』

獨語	dú yǔ	monologue
不耐煩	bú nàifán	impatient
額角	éjiǎo	temples
傷疤	shāngbā	scar
含胡	hánhú	evasively
依	yǐ	to submit
扭不過	niǔ bú guò	to fail to win the argument
推說	tuīshuō	to blame it on
蹙縮	cùsuō	puckered
核桃	hútáo	walnut
乾枯	gānkū	dried and shrivelled
局促	júcù	uneasy, embarrassed, a feeling of constraint
不合算	bù hésuàn	it wasn't worth it
詭祕	guǐmì	as if harbouring a mischievous secret
再一強	zài yì jiang	if you been stubborn and held out longer
索性	suǒxìng	might as well go the whole hog
過活	guò huó	to live
落一件大罪名	luò yí jiàn dà zuìmíng	to gain the stigma of having committed a serious offense
陰司	yīnsī	the underworld
閻羅大王	yánluó dà wáng	one of the kings of the underworld (Buddhist)
鋸	jù	to saw; saw

　　她臉上就顯出恐怖的神色來，這是在山村裏所未曾知道的。

　　『我想，你不如及早抵當。你到土地廟裏去捐一條門檻，當作你的替身，給千人踏，萬人跨，贖了這一世的罪名，免得死了去受苦。』

　　她當時並不回答什麼話，但大約非常苦悶了，第二天早上起來的時候，兩眼上便都圍着大黑圈。早飯之後，她便到鎮的西頭的土地廟裏去求捐門檻。廟祝起初執意不允許，直到她急得流淚，纔勉强答應了。價目是大錢十二千。

　　她久已不和人們交口，因爲阿毛的故事是早被大家厭棄了的；但自從和柳媽談了天，似乎又即傳揚開去，許多人都發生了新趣味，又來逗她說話了。至于題目，那自然是換了一個新樣，專在她額上的傷疤。

　　『祥林嫂，我問你：你那時怎麼竟肯了？』一個說。

　　『唉，可惜，白撞了這一下。』一個看着她的疤，應和道。

　　她大約從他們的笑容和聲調上，也知道是在嘲笑她，所以總是瞪着眼睛，不說一句話，後來連頭也不回了。她整日緊閉了嘴唇，頭上帶着大家以爲恥辱的記號的那傷痕，默默的跑街，掃地，洗菜，淘米。快夠一年，她纔從四嬸手裏支取了歷來積存的工錢，換算了十二元鷹洋，請假到鎮的西頭去。但不到一頓飯時候，她便回來，神氣很舒暢，眼光也分外有神，高

抵當	dǐdàng	to pay the penalty
土地	tǔdì	the god of the local area
捐	jüān	to donate
替身	tìshēn	substitute
踏	tà	to tread on
跨	kuà	to step over
贖	shú	to redeem one's offence by the payment of a fine
免得	miǎnde	to save yourself from
廟祝	miàozhù	keeper of the temple
執意	zhíyì	adamant
允許	yǔnxǔ	to accede to a request
勉强	miǎnqiǎng	with reluctance
價目	jiàmù	price
交口	jiāokǒu	to enter into conversation with
傳揚	chuányáng	to spread far and wide
逗	dòu	to tease into doing something
白	bái	for nothing
應和	yìnghè	to echo
跑街	pǎojiē	to go on errands
歷來	lìlái	all along
積存	jīcún	to deposit and accumulate
換算	huànsuàn	to change into
鷹洋	yìngyáng	Mexican dollars
請假	qǐng jià	ask for time off

興似的對四嬸說，自己已經在土地廟捐了門檻了。

　　冬至的祭祖時節，她做得更出力，看四嬸裝好祭品，和阿牛將桌子擡到堂屋中央，她便坦然的去拿酒盃和筷子。

　　『你放着罷，祥林嫂！』四嬸慌忙大聲說。

　　她像是受了炮烙似的縮手，臉色同時變作灰黑，也不再去取燭臺，只是失神的站着。直到四叔上香的時候，教她走開，她纔走開。這一回她的變化非常大，第二天，不但眼睛窈陷下去，連精神也更不濟了。而且很膽怯，不獨怕暗夜，怕黑影，即使看見人，雖是自己的主人，也總惴惴的，有如在白天出穴游行的小鼠；否則獃坐着，直是一個木偶人。不半年，頭髮也花白起來了，記性尤其壞，甚而至于常常忘卻了去淘米。

　　『祥林嫂怎麼這樣了？倒不如那時不留她。』四嬸有時當面就這樣說，似乎是警告她。

　　然而她總如此，全不見有怜悧起來的希望。他們于是想打發她走了，教她回到衛老婆子那里去。但當我還在魯鎮的時候，不過單是這樣說；看現在的情狀，可見後來終于實行了。然而她是從四叔家出去就成了乞丐的呢，還是先到衛老婆子家然後再成乞丐的呢？那我可不知道。

　　我給那些因爲在近旁而極響的爆竹聲驚醒，看見豆一般大的黃色的燈火光，接着又聽得畢畢剝剝的鞭炮，是四叔家正在『祝福』了；知道已是五更將近時

坦然	tǎnrán	without a worry
炮烙	pàoluò	branding iron
失神	shīshén	mindless, vacant
上香	shàng xiāng	to offer up the incense
窈（凹）陷	āoxiàn	sunk
精神不濟	jīngshén bú jì	lacking in energy, easily tired
膽怯	dǎnqiè	timid
惴惴	zhuìzhuì	apprehensive
尤其	yóuqí	particularly
恰悧起來	línglì qǐ lái	to perk up
打發	dǎfā	to send someone on his way
畢畢剝剝	bìbì bōbō	crackling sound (onomat.)
鞭炮	biānpào	string of crackers

候。我在蒙朧中，又隱約聽到遠處的爆竹聲聯緜不斷，
似乎合成一天音響的濃雲，夾着團團飛舞的雪花，擁
抱了全市鎮。我在這繁響的擁抱中，也懶散而且舒適，
從白天以至初夜的疑慮，全給祝福的空氣一掃而空了，
只覺得天地聖衆歆享了牲醴和香煙，都醉醺醺的在空
中蹣跚，豫備給魯鎮的人們以無限的幸福。

隱約	yǐnyüē	faintly, can be barely made out
聯縣不斷	liánmián bú duàn	without a break
團團	tuántuán	round and round
擁抱	yōngbào	to embrace; embrace
懶散	lǎnsǎn	lethargic
舒適	shūshì	comfortable
歆享	xīnxiǎng	(class.) to enjoy (offerings)
牲醴	shēng lǐ	sacrfiicial animals and wine
蹣跚	pánshān	to stagger
無限	wúxiàn	unlimited
幸福	xìngfú	happiness

在酒樓上

我從北地向東南旅行，繞道訪了我的家鄉，就到S城。這城離我的故鄉不過三十里，坐了小船，小半天可到，我曾在這里的學校裏當過一年的教員。深冬雪後，風景淒清，懶散和懷舊的心緒聯結起來，我竟暫寓在S城的洛思旅館裏了；這旅館是先前所沒有的。城圈本不大，尋訪了幾個以爲可以會見的舊同事，一個也不在，早不知散到那里去了；經過學校的門口，也改換了名稱和模樣，于我很生疏。不到兩個時辰，我的意興早已索然，頗悔此來爲多事了。

我所住的旅館是租房不賣飯的，飯菜必須另外叫來，但又無味，入口如嚼泥土。窗外只有漬痕斑駁的牆壁，帖着枯死的莓苔；上面是鉛色的天，白皚皚的絕無精采，而且微雪又飛舞起來了。我午餐本沒有飽，又沒有可以消遣的事情，便很自然的想到先前有一家很熟識的小酒樓，叫一石居的，算來離旅館並不遠。我于是立即鎖了房門，出街向那酒樓去。其實也無非想姑且逃避客中的無聊，並不專爲買醉。一石居是在的，狹小陰溼的店面和破舊的招牌都依舊；但從掌櫃以至堂倌卻已沒有一個熟人，我在這一石居中也完全成了生客。然而我終于跨上那走熟的屋角的扶梯去了，由此徑到小樓上。上面也依然是五張小板桌；獨有原

在酒樓上　Zài jiǔlóu shàng

北地	běi dì	northern parts
繞道	rào dào	to make a detour
小半天	xiǎo bàn tiān	less than half a day
淒清	qīqing	bleak
懷舊	huái jiù	nostalgic
聯結起來	liánjié qǐ lái	to combine
城圈	chéngquān	the confines of the city
同事	tóngshì	colleagues
名稱	míngchēng	the name it is known by
生疏	shēngshū	unfamiliar
時辰	shíchén	period of two hours
意興索然	yìxìng suǒrán	to feel flat, all the enthusiasm gone
此來	cǐ lái	this trip, this visit
漬痕	zì hén	stain
斑駁	bānbó	patchy (in colour)
帖（貼）着	tiē zhe	to be plastered with
莓苔	méitái	moss
鉛	qiān	lead
白皚皚	báiǎiǎi	dead white
本	běn	in the first instance
消遣	xiāoqiǎn	pastime
酒樓	jiǔlóu	restaurant
算來	suàn lái	when you come to reckon it
無非	wúfēi	for no other purpose than; is none other than
姑且	gūqiě	for the moment
客中	kèzhōng	while away from home as a traveller
無聊	wúliáo	ennui
買醉	mǎizuì	to get out and get drunk
狹小	xiáxiǎo	pokey
陰溼	yīnshī	dark and damp
招牌	zhāopái	signboard
堂倌	tángguān	waiter
生客	shēng kè	stranger (customer, visitor)
扶梯	fútī	stairs with handrail
徑	jìng	straight (to, up)

是木櫺的後窗卻換嵌了玻璃。

　　『一斤紹酒。——菜?十個油豆腐，辣醬要多！』

　　我一面說給跟我上來的堂倌聽，一面向後窗走，就在靠窗的一張桌旁坐下了。樓上『空空如也』，任我揀得最好的坐位：可以眺望樓下的廢園。這園大概是不屬于酒家的，我先前也曾眺望過許多回，有時也在雪天裏。但現在從慣于北方的眼睛看來，卻很值得驚異了：幾株老梅竟鬬雪開着滿樹的繁花，彷彿毫不以深冬爲意；倒塌的亭子邊還有一株山茶樹，從暗綠的密葉裏顯出十幾朵紅花來，赫赫的在雪中明得如火，憤怒而且傲慢，如蔑視遊人的甘心于遠行。我這時又忽地想到這里積雪的滋潤，著物不去，晶瑩有光，不比朔雪的粉一般乾，大風一吹，便飛得滿空如煙霧。……

　　『客人，酒。……』

　　堂倌懶懶的說着，放下杯，筷，酒壺和碗碟，酒到了。我轉臉向了板桌，排好器具，斟出酒來。覺得北方固不是我的舊鄉，但南來又只能算一個客子，無論那邊的乾雪怎樣紛飛，這里的柔雪又怎樣的依戀，于我都沒有什麼關係了。我略帶些哀愁，然而很舒服的呷一口酒。酒味很純正；油豆腐也煮得十分好；可惜辣醬太淡薄，本來S城人是不懂得喫辣的。

　　大概是因爲正在下午的緣故罷，這雖說是酒樓，卻毫無酒樓氣，我已經喝下三杯酒去了，而我以外還是四張空板桌。我看着廢園，漸漸的感到孤獨，但又不願有別的酒客上來。偶然聽得樓梯上腳步響，便不

木櫺	mùlíng	lattice
嵌	qiàn	inlay
辣醬	là jiàng	hot sauce
空空如也	kōng kōng rú yě	empty (facetious)
眺望	tiàowàng	to gaze out at (view)
廢園	fèiyüan	disused garden
值得驚異	zhí de jīng yì	worth being surprised at
闘雪	dòu xüě	to vie with the snow (poet. cliché)
不以爲意	bù yǐ wéi yì	not a bit concerned
倒塌	dǎotā	to collapse
山茶	shānchá	camellia
密	mì	thick, dense
赫赫的	hèhè di	vividly
傲慢	àomàn	haughty
蔑視	mièshì	to look down upon
甘心	gānxīn	willing, without complaint
滋潤	zīrùn	to moisten and so having a nourishing effect on
着物不去	zhuó wù bú qù	not to come off once it sticks on to something
晶瑩	jīngyíng	glistening
朔雪	shuò xüě	snow from the cold north
斟	zhēn	to pour (drink)
固	gù	it goes without saying
客子	kèzǐ	(class.) traveller away from his native place
依戀	yīliàn	to cling to lingeringly
呷	xiā	to sip
純正	chúnzhèng	pure and genuine
淡薄	dànbó	thin, weak

由的有些懊惱，待到看見是堂倌，纔又安心了，這樣
的又喝了兩杯酒。

　　我想，這回定是酒客了，因爲聽得那脚步聲比堂
倌的要緩得多。約略料他走完了樓梯的時候，我便害
怕似的擡頭去看這無干的同伴，同時也就喫驚的站起
來。我竟不料在這里意外的遇見朋友了，──假如他
現在還許我稱他爲朋友。那上來的分明是我的舊同窗，
也是做教員時代的舊同事，面貌雖然頗有些改變，但
一見也就認識，獨有行動卻變得格外迂緩，很不像當
年敏捷精悍的呂緯甫了。

　　『阿，──緯甫，是你麼？我萬想不到會在這里
遇見你。』

　　『阿阿，是你？我也萬想不到……』

　　我就邀他同坐，但他似乎略略躊躕之後，方纔坐
下來。我起先很以爲奇，接着便有些悲傷，而且不快
了。細看他相貌，也還是亂蓬蓬的鬚髮；蒼白的長方
臉，然而衰瘦了。精神很沈靜，或者卻是頹唐；又濃
又黑的眉毛底下的眼睛也失了精采，但當他緩緩的四
顧的時候，卻對廢園忽地閃出我在學校時代常常看見
的射人的光來。

　　『我們，』我高興的，然而頗不自然的說，『我
們這一別，怕有十年了罷。我早知道你在濟南，可是
實在懶得太難，終于沒有寫一封信。……』

　　『彼此都一樣。可是現在我在太原了，已經兩年
多，和我的母親。我回來接她的時候，知道你早搬走

懊惱	àonǎo	vexed
緩	huǎn	slow
約略	yüēlüè	roughly
無干	wúgān	nothing to do with
同伴	tóngbàn	companion
同窗	tóngchuāng	fellow student of the same class
迂緩	yūhüǎn	slow
敏捷	mǐnjié	quick
精悍	jīnghàn	forceful
邀	yāo	to invite
起先	qǐxiān	at first
不快	búkuài	displeased
長方	chángfāng	rectangular
衰瘦	shuāishòu	grown old and thin
沈靜	chénjìng	quiet, subdued
頹唐	tuítáng	dejected
四顧	sì gù	to look all round
射	shè	to shoot an arrow, to shoot out, to shoot at, to pierce
不自然	bú zìrán	awkward; unnatural, self-conscious
怕	pà	it must be that

了，搬得很乾淨。』

『你在太原做什麼呢？』我問。

『敎書，在一個同鄉的家裏。』

『這以前呢？』

『這以前麼？』他從衣袋裏掏出一支煙卷來，點了火啣在嘴裏，看着噴出的煙霧，沈思似的說，『無非做了些無聊的事情，等于什麼也沒有做。』

他也問我別後的景況；我一面告訴他一個大概，一面叫堂倌先取杯筷來，使他先喝着我的酒，然後再去添二斤。其間還點菜，我們先前原是毫不客氣的，但此刻卻推讓起來了，終于說不淸那一樣是誰點的，就從堂倌的口頭報告上指定了四樣菜：茴香豆，凍肉，油豆腐，靑魚乾。

『我一回來，就想到我可笑。』他一手擎着煙卷，一隻手扶着酒杯，似笑非笑的向我說。『我在少年時，看見蜂子或蠅子停在一個地方，給什麼來一嚇，即刻飛去了，但是飛了一個小圈子，便又回來停在原地點，便以爲這實在很可笑，也可憐。可不料現在我自己也飛回來了，不過繞了一點小圈子。又不料你也回來了。你不能飛得更遠些麼？』

『這難說，大約也不外乎繞點小圈子罷。』我也似笑非笑的說。『但是你爲什麼飛回來的呢？』

『也還是爲了無聊的事。』他一口喝乾了一杯酒，吸幾口煙，眼睛略爲張大了。『無聊的。——但是我們就談談罷。』

煙卷（捲）	yānjüǎn	cigarettes
沈思	chénsī	deep in thought
無非	wúfēi	simply, what except
無聊	wúliáo	futile
等于	děngyú	equivalent to
點菜	diǎncài	to select dishes from the menu
推讓	tūiràng	to let the other person go first
說不清	shuō bù qīng	difficult to say
口頭	kōutóu	oral
凍肉	dòngròu	jellied meat
擎	qíng	to hold up (as in case of a torch)
扶着	fú zhe	with his fingers round
蜂子	fēngzǐ	bee
蠅子	yíngzǐ	a fly
不外乎	búwàihū	does not go beyond, you know the kind of thing

　　堂倌搬上新添的酒菜來，排滿了一桌，樓上又添了煙氣和油豆腐的熱氣，彷彿熱鬧起來了；樓外的雪也越加紛紛的下。

　　『你也許本來知道，』他接着說，『我曾經有一個小兄弟，是三歲上死掉的，就葬在這鄉下。我連他的模樣都記不清楚了，但聽母親說，是一個很可愛念的孩子，和我也很相投，至今她提起來還似乎要下淚。今年春天，一個堂兄就來了一封信，說他的墳邊已經漸漸的浸了水，不久怕要陷入河裏去了，須得趕緊去設法。母親一知道就很着急，幾乎幾夜睡不着，——她又自己能看信的。然而我能有什麼法子呢？沒有錢，沒有工夫：當時什麼法也沒有。

　　『一直挨到現在，趁着年假的閒空，我纔得回南給他來遷葬。』他又喝乾一酒杯，看着窗外，說，『這在那邊那里能如此呢？積雪裏會有花，雪地下會不凍。就在前天，我在城裏買了一口小棺材，——因爲我豫料那地下的應該早已朽爛了，——帶着棉絮和被褥，僱了四個土工，下鄉遷葬去。我當時忽而很高興，願意掘一回墳，願意一見我那曾經和我很親睦的小兄弟的骨殖：這些事我生平都沒有經歷過。到得墳地，果然，河水只是咬進來，離墳已不到二尺遠。可憐的墳，兩年沒有培土，也平下去了。我站在雪中，決然的指着他對土工說，「掘開來！」我實在是一個庸人，我這時覺得我的聲音有些希奇，這命令也是一個在我一生中最爲偉大的命令。但土工們卻毫不駭怪，就動

紛紛	fēnfēn	(to come down) in a shower
可愛念	kě àiniàn	lovable
相投	xiāngtóu	to get on well together
浸了水	jìn le shuǐ	to come under water
設法	shèfǎ	to do something about
着急	zhāo jí	agitated
幾乎	jīhū	almost
挨到	ái dào	to drag on till
年假	niánjià	New Year Vacation
遷葬	qiānzàng	to re-bury in another place
會	huì	it can happen
凍	dòng	to freeze
豫料	yùliào	to reckon, anticipate
朽爛	xiǔlàn	to rot
棉絮	mián xù	cotton wool
被褥	bèirù	bedding
土工	tǔ gōng	diggers
親睦	cīnmù	close, dear to, on good terms with, friendly with
骨殖	gǔshi	skeleton, remains
只是	zhǐshì	to keep on at it
培土	péi tǔ	to bank up with earth
平下去	píng xià qù	to flatten down
決然	jüérán	decisively
庸人	yóngrén	common, unremarkable, sort of person
駭怪	hàiguài	startled or surprised
動手	dòng shǒu	to set to work

手掘下去了。待到掘着壙穴，我便過去看，果然，棺木已經快要爛盡了，只剩下一堆木絲和小木片。我的心顫動着，自去撥開這些，很小心的，要看一看我的小兄弟。然而出乎意外！被褥，衣服，骨骼，什麼也沒有。我想，這些都消盡了，向來聽說最難爛的是頭髮，也許還有罷。我便伏下去，在該是枕頭所在的泥土裏仔仔細細的看，也沒有。蹤影全無！』

　　我忽而看見他眼圈微紅了，但立即知道是有了酒意。他總不很喫菜，單是把酒不停的喝，早喝了一斤多，神情和舉動都活潑起來，漸近于先前所見的呂緯甫了。我叫堂倌再添二斤酒，然後回轉身，也擎着酒杯，正對面默默的聽着。

　　『其實，這本已可以不必再遷，只要平了土，賣掉棺材，就此完事了的。我去賣棺材雖然有些離奇，但只要價錢極便宜，原鋪子就許要，至少總可以撈回幾文酒錢來。但我不這樣，我仍然鋪好被褥，用棉花裏了些他先前身體所在的地方的泥土，包起來，裝在新棺材裏，運到我父親埋着的墳地上，在他墳旁埋掉了。因為外面用磚墎，昨天又忙了我大半天：監工。但這樣總算完結了一件事，足夠去騙騙我的母親，使她安心些。——阿阿，你這樣的看我，你怪我何以和先前太不相同了麼？是的，我也還記得我們同到城隍廟裏去拔掉神像的鬍子的時候，連日議論些改革中國的方法以至于打起來的時候。但我現在就是這樣了，敷敷衍衍，模模胡胡。我有時自己也想到，倘若先前

壙穴	kuàngxüè	the space for the coffin
木絲	mù sī	shreds of wood
木片	mù piàn	slithers of wood
出乎意外	chū hū yì wài	to be totally unexpected
骨骼	gǔgé	skeleton
酒意	jiǔyì	signs of the wine taking effect
神情	shénqíng	expression (on face)
舉動	jǔdòng	gestures, movements
本已＝本來已經		
撈回	lāo huí	to get back
棉花	miánhuā	cotton wool
用磚鄩	yòng zhuān guō	to wall up with bricks
監工	jiān gōng	to oversee the workmen
先前	xiānqián	the old days
城隍	chénghuáng	guardian deity of a city
神像	shén xiàng	the images of the gods
議論	yìlùn	to discuss
打起來	dǎ qǐ lái	to come to blows
敷衍	fūyǎn	just to cope
模胡	móhú	vague 〔？＝馬虎〕 perfunctory

的朋友看見我，怕會不認我做朋友了。——然而我現
在就是這樣。』

　　他又掏出一支煙卷來，唧在嘴裏，點了火。

　　『看你的神情，你似乎還有些期望我，——我現
在自然麻木得多了，但是有些事也還看得出。這使我
很感激，然而也使我很不安：怕我終于辜負了至今還
對我懷着好意的老朋友。……』他忽而停住了，吸幾
口煙，纔又慢慢的說，『正在今天，剛在我到這一石
居來之前，也就做了一件無聊事，然而也是我自己願
意做的。我先前的東邊的鄰居叫長富，是一個船戶。
他有一個女兒叫阿順，你那時到我家裏來，也許見過
的，但你一定沒有留心，因爲那時她還小。後來她也
長得並不好看，不過是平常的瘦瘦的瓜子臉，黃臉皮；
獨有眼睛非常大，睫毛也很長，眼白又靑得如夜的晴
天，而且是北方的無風的晴天，這里的就沒有那麼明
淨了。她很能幹，十多歲沒了母親，招呼兩個小弟妹
都靠她；又得服侍父親，事事都周到；也經濟，家計
倒漸漸的穩當起來了。鄰居幾乎沒有一個不誇獎她，
連長富也時常說些感激的話。這一次我動身回來的時
候，我的母親又記得她了，老年人記性眞長久。她說
她曾經知道順姑因爲看見誰的頭上戴着紅的剪絨花，
自己也想有一朵，弄不到，哭了，哭了小半夜，就挨
了她父親的一頓打，後來眼眶還紅腫了兩三天。這種
剪絨花是外省的東西，S 城裏尚且買不出，她那里想
得到手呢？趁我這一次回南的便，便叫我買兩朵去送

期望我	qī wàng wǒ	entertain expectations of me
麻木	mámù	numbed
看得出	kàn de chū	to make out
辜負	gūfù	to let down
好意	hǎoyì	good will, good intentions
船戶	chuánhù	boatman
留心	líuxīn	to pay attention
長	zhǎng	to grow
長得好看＝生得好看		to be good looking
瓜子臉	guāzǐ liǎn	face the shape of a melon seed
黃臉皮	huáng liǎnpí	sallow complexion
睫毛	jiémáo	eyelashes
眼白	yǎnbái	whites of the eyes
晴天	qíngtiān	cloudless sky
而且	érqiě	at that
明淨	míngjìng	clear, spotless
招呼	zhāohū	to look after
服侍	fúshì	to look after (superior, senior)
周到	zhōudào	circumspect, to have thought of everything
經濟	jīngjì	frugal, economical; economy, economics
家計	jiājì	family finances
穩當	wěndàng	secure
誇獎	kuājiǎng	praise
剪絨花	jiǎnróng huā	flower cut out of velvet
眼眶	yǎnkuàng	rims of the eyes

她。

　　『我對于這差使倒並不以爲煩厭，反而很喜歡；爲阿順，我實在還有些願意出力的意思的。前年，我回來接我母親的時候，有一天，長富正在家，不知怎的我和他閒談起來了。他便要請我喫點心，蕎麥粉，並且告訴我所加的是白糖。你想，家裏能有白糖的船戶，可見決不是一個窮船戶了，所以他也喫得很闊綽。我被勸不過，答應了，但要求只要用小碗。他也很識世故，便囑咐阿順說，「他們文人，是不會喫東西的。你就用小碗，多加糖！」然而等到調好端來的時候，仍然使我喫一嚇，是一大碗，足夠我喫一天。但是和長富喫的一碗比起來，我的也確乎算小碗。我生平沒有喫過蕎麥粉，這回一嘗，實在不可口，卻是非常甜。我漫然的喫了幾口，就想不喫了，然而無意中，忽然間看見阿順遠遠的站在屋角裏，就使我立刻消失了放下碗筷的勇氣。我看她的神情，是害怕而且希望，大約怕自己調得不好，願我們喫得有味。我知道如果剩下大半碗來，一定要使她很失望，而且很抱歉。我于是同時決心，放開喉嚨灌下去了，幾乎喫得和長富一樣快。我由此纔知道硬喫的苦痛，我只記得還做孩子時候的喫盡一碗拌着驅除蛔蟲藥粉的沙糖纔有這樣難。然而我毫不抱怨，因爲她過來收拾空碗時候的忍着的得意的笑容，已儘夠賠償我的苦痛而有餘了。所以我這一夜雖然飽脹得睡不穩，又做了一大串惡夢，也還是祝讚她一生幸福，願世界爲她變好。然而這些意思

差使（事）	chāishi	errand
煩厭	fányàn	bothersome
蕎麥粉	qiáomài fěn	buckwheat flour
闊綽	kuòchuò	posh, in style
被勸不過	bèi quàn bú guò	could not withstand the persuasion
要求	yāoqiú	to request
識世故	shí shìgù	worldly, understanding
文人	wénrén	man of letters, educated man
囑咐	zhǔfu	to charge someone with a task
調	tiáo	to mix
不可口	bù kěkǒu	unpalatable
漫然	mànrán	casually
無意中	wúyì zhōng	by chance
消失	xiāoshī	to lose
勇氣	yǒngqì	courage
抱歉	bàoqiàn	apologetic
硬喫	yìng chī	forced feeding
拌着	bàn zhe	mixed with
驅除	qūchú	to get rid of
蛔蟲	huíchóng	tapeworms
抱怨	bàoyuàn	to complain
忍着	rěn zhe	trying to stifle
得意	déyì	proud, to be full of one's success
賠償	péicháng	to repay, to recompense
飽脹	bǎo zhàng	puffed
惡夢	è mèng	nightmare
祝讚	zhùzàn	to bless

也不過是我的那些舊日的夢的痕迹，即刻就自笑，接着也就忘卻了。

　　『我先前並不知道她曾經爲了一朵剪絨花挨打，但因爲母親一說起，便也記得了蕎麥粉的事，意外的勤快起來了。我先在太原城裏搜求了一遍，都沒有；一直到濟南……』

　　窗外沙沙的一陣聲響，許多積雪從被他壓彎了的一枝山茶樹上滑下去了，樹枝筆挺的伸直，更顯出烏油油的肥葉和血紅的花來。天空的鉛色來得更濃；小鳥雀啾唧的叫着，大概黃昏將近，地面又全罩了雪，尋不出什麼食糧，都趕早回巢來休息了。

　　『一直到了濟南，』他向窗外看了一回，轉身喝乾一杯酒，又吸幾口煙，接着說。『我纔買到剪絨花。我也不知道使她挨打的是不是這一種，總之是絨做的罷了。我也不知道她喜歡深色還是淺色，就買了一朵大紅的，一朵粉紅的，都帶到這裏來。

　　『就是今天午後，我一喫完飯，便去看長富，我爲此特地耽擱了一天。他的家倒還在，只是看去很有些晦氣色了，但這恐怕不過是我自己的感覺。他的兒子和第二個女兒——阿昭，都站在門口，大了。阿昭長得全不像她姊姊，簡直像一個鬼，但是看見我走向她家，便飛奔的逃進屋裏去。我就問那小子，知道長富不在家。「你的大姊呢？」他立刻瞪起眼睛，連聲問我尋她什麼事，而且惡狠狠的似乎就要撲過來，咬我。我支吾着退走了，我現在是敷敷衍衍……

勤快	qínkuài	eagerness, alacrity
搜求	sōuqiú	to search for
一直到	yì zhí dào	not until
筆挺	bǐtǐng	erect
烏油油	wūyóuyóu	sleek
啾唧	jiūjí	chirping
粉紅	fěnhóng	pink
躭擱	dāngē	to delay
晦氣	huìqì	aura of bad luck
感覺	gǎnjüé	feeling, sensing
全不像	quán bú xiàng	not at all like
小子	xiǎozǐ	little fellow (disparaging)
連聲	lián shēng	repeatedly
惡狠狠	è hěn hěn	angrily, fiercely
撲過來	pū guò lái	to rush over, to pounce upon

　　『你不知道，我可是比先前更怕去訪人了。因為我已經深知道自己之討厭，連自己也討厭，又何必明知故犯的去使人暗暗地不快呢？然而這回的差使是不能不辦妥的，所以想了一想，終于回到就在斜對門的柴店裏。店主的母親，老發奶奶，倒也還在，而且也還認識我，居然將我邀進店裏坐去了。我們寒暄幾句之後，我就說明了回到 S 城和尋長富的緣故。不料她歎息說：

　　『「可惜順姑沒有福氣戴這剪絨花了。」

　　『她于是詳細的告訴我，說是「大約從去年春天以來，她就見得黃瘦，後來忽而常常下淚了，問她緣故又不說；有時還整夜的哭，哭得長富也忍不住生氣，罵她年紀大了，發了瘋。可是一到秋初，起先不過小傷風，終于躺倒了，從此就起不來。直到咽氣的前幾天，纔肯對長富說，她早就像她母親一樣，不時的吐紅和流夜汗。但是瞞着，怕他因此要擔心。有一夜，她的伯伯長庚又來硬借錢，——這是常有的事，——她不給，長庚就冷笑着說：你不要驕氣，你的男人比我還不如！她從此就發了愁，又怕羞，不好問，只好哭。長富趕緊將她的男人怎樣的掙氣的話說給她聽，那裏還來得及？況且她也不信，反而說：好在我已經這樣，什麼也不要緊了。」

　　『她還說，「如果她的男人真比長庚不如，那就真可怕呵！比不上一個偷雞賊，那是什麼東西呢？然而他來送殮的時候，我是親眼看見他的，衣服很乾淨，

討厭	tǎoyàn	unattractive
明知故犯	míng zhī gù fàn	to do something deliberately knowing full well what the outcome is
暗暗地	ànàn de	in their hearts
辦妥	bàn tuǒ	to manage satisfactorily
居然	jūrán	actually (unexpected success)
忍不住	rěn bú zhù	unable to restrain oneself
發了瘋	fā le feng	to have gone mad
傷風	shāng fēng	cold
躺倒	tǎng dǎo	to take to bed
咽氣	yàn qì	to breathe one's last
不時	bù shí	from time to time
吐紅	tùhóng	to spit blood
擔心	dānxīn	to worry
硬	yìng	not to take 'no' for an answer
驕氣	jiāoqì	stuck up
趕緊	gǎnjǐn	to hasten to
掙（爭）氣	zhēngqì	one to be proud of, not to let someone down
那里還來得及	nǎ lǐ hái lái de jí	it was too late
好在	hǎozài	it is a good thing that (cf. 幸虧)
不要緊	bú yàojǐn	unimportant
偷雞賊	tōu jī zéi	a petty thief
送殮	sòng liàn	to attend the encoffinning ceremony

人也體面；還眼淚汪汪的說，自己撐了半世小船，苦熬苦省的積起錢來聘了一個女人，偏偏又死掉了。可見他實在是一個好人，長庚說的全是誑。只可惜順姑竟會相信那樣的賊骨頭的誑話，白送了性命。——但這也不能去怪誰，只能怪順姑自己沒有這一份好福氣。」

　　『那倒也罷，我的事情又完了。但是帶在身邊的兩朵剪絨花怎麼辦呢？好，我就託她送了阿昭。這阿昭一見我就飛跑，大約將我當作一隻狼或是什麼，我實在不願意去送她。——但是我也就送她了，對母親只要說阿順見了喜歡的了不得就是。這些無聊的事算什麼？只要模模胡胡。模模胡胡的過了新年，仍舊教我的「子曰詩云」去。』

　　『你教的是「子曰詩云」麼？』我覺得奇異，便問。

　　『自然。你還以為教的是ＡＢＣＤ麼？我先是兩個學生，一個讀《詩經》，一個讀《孟子》。新近又添了一個，女的，讀《女兒經》。連算學也不教，不是我不教，他們不要教。』

　　『我實在料不到你倒去教這類的書，……』

　　『他們的老子要他們讀這些；我是別人，無乎不可的。這些無聊的事算什麼？只要隨隨便便，……』

　　他滿臉已經通紅，似乎很有些醉，但眼光卻又消沈下去了。我微微的歎息，一時沒有話可說。樓梯上一陣亂響，擁上幾個酒客來：當頭的是矮子，擁腫的圓臉；第二個是長的，在臉上很惹眼的顯出一個紅鼻

體面	tǐmiàn	presentable
淚汪汪	lèiwāngwāng	full of tears
苦熬苦省	kǔ aó kǔ shěng	to scrimp and save
聘	pìng	to betroth
偏偏又死掉了	piān piān yòu sǐ diào le	it would have to happen that she died
誆	kuáng	lies
賊骨頭	zéi gǔtóu	thief (abusive)
子曰詩云	zǐ yūē shǐ yǘn	The Master said, the Book of Odes has it, i.e., the classics
女兒經	nǚ ér jīng	book of maxims for girls of unknown authorship existing in more than one version
算學	suànxüé	mathematics
老子	lǎozǐ	father
別人	biérén	outsiders
無乎不可	wú hū bù kě、	easy going
隨隨便便	suísuí biànbiàn	casual
消沈	xiāochén	to subside
一時	yǐ shí	for a time
擁上	yōng shàng	to rush up in a crowd
當頭	dāng tóu	at the head
矮子	ǎizǐ	short man
擁(臃)腫	yōngzhǒng	swollen, bulging
惹眼	rěyǎn	attracts attention, conspicuous

子；此後還有人，一疊連的走得小樓都發抖。我轉眼去看呂緯甫，他也正轉眼來看我，我就叫堂倌算酒賬。

『你藉此還可以支持生活麼？』我一面準備走，一面問。

『是的。──我每月有二十元，也不大能夠敷衍。』

『那麼，你以後豫備怎麼辦呢？』

『以後？──我不知道。你看我們那時豫想的事可有一件如意？我現在什麼也不知道，連明天怎樣也不知道，連後一分……』

堂倌送上賬來，交給我；他也不像初到時候的謙虛了，只向我看了一眼，便吸煙，聽憑我付了賬。

我們一同走出店門，他所住的旅館和我的方向正相反，就在門口分別了。我獨自向着自己的旅館走，寒風和雪片撲在臉上，倒覺得很爽快。見天色已是黃昏，和屋宇和街道都織在密雪的純白而不定的羅網裏。

一疊連	yì dié lián	one upon another
樓	lóu	the upstairs part of a building
算賬	suàn zhàng	to make up the bill
藉此	jiè cǐ	by means of this
支持	zhīchí	to support
準備	zhǔnbì	ready to
敷衍	fūyǎn	to manage
豫想	yùxiǎng	to envisage
一分	yì fēn	one minute
謙虛	qiānxū	diffident, modest (here used to mean "to stand on ceremony")
聽憑	tīngpíng	to leave someone to do as he pleases
方向	fāngxiàng	direction
相反	xiāngfǎn	opposite
撲	pū	to waft against
屋宇	wūyǔ	buildings, dwellings
不定的	bú dìng de	shifting
羅網	luówǎng	net